THE QUIET FIELDS

Fennel's Journal

No. 7

THE QUIET FIELDS

By

Fennel Hudson

2025

FENNEL'S PRIORY LIMITED

Published by Fennel's Priory Limited

www.fennelspriory.com

First shared as handwritten letters in 2011
Limited edition magazine published in 2012
eBook published in 2013
This first edition hardback published in 2025

A CIP catalogue record for this book
is available from the British Library.

ISBN 978-1-909947-26-9

Available to purchase in other formats at
www.fennelspriory.com

Designed and typeset in 12pt Adobe Garamond Premier Pro.

CONTENTS

STOP – UNPLUG – ESCAPE – ENJOY

This book, and the series to which it belongs, is about freedom. It's also about the adventures to be had when pursuing one's dreams, developing and communicating one's self, and striving for a slow-paced rural life.

Fennel's Journal is your opportunity to take time out from the stresses of modern living, to stop the wheels for a while, unplug from the daily grind, escape to a quiet and peaceful place, and enjoy the simple life. Because of this, it should ideally be read in a distraction-free and relaxing environment: your 'safe place' where you can savour quality time and, if possible, delight in the beauty of the countryside.

That's why this book is pocket-sized, has a special waxy cover, and is printed using waterproof ink. It's designed to be taken with you on your travels. Don't store it in pristine condition upon a bookshelf; allow it to reflect the adventures you've had. Use a leaf as a bookmark and annotate the pages with ideas of how you will honour your right to 'never do anything that offends your soul'.

The more mud-splattered, grass-stained, and ink-scribbled this book becomes, the more you've demonstrated your ability to pursue a contented country life. So go on: live your life, be authentic, and always remember to 'Stop – Unplug – Escape – Enjoy'.

"The most precious places in the English landscape are those secretive corners where you find only elder trees, nettles and dreams."

'BB'

INTRODUCTION

1981: the year that gave us such pleasures as *Donkey Kong* and *MTV*, when British band *Bucks Fizz* won the Eurovision Song Contest and everybody started running (so very slowly) to watch *Chariots of Fire* at the cinema; when America launched its first Space Shuttle and Great Britain celebrated the wedding of Prince Charles and Lady Diana. But alas, Mohammad Ali retired, as did Tom Baker from his role as Doctor Who (I never quite got over that). And Britney Spears, Justin Timberlake and Paris Hilton were born. But let's not get too depressed. 1981 was the year when *The Hitchhiker's Guide to the Galaxy* was aired on television and a rather nice book about the English countryside was published.

The book to which I refer was entitled *The Quiet Fields*. Denys Watkins-Pitchford, also known as 'BB', wrote it in his 76th year and as such it benefits from his years of experience and lifelong interest in wildlife. But what makes it so special is that most of the book is about the wildlife that visits his garden, which illustrates how the naturalist doesn't have to venture far to discover things of interest. The book is factual and succinctly written for those who understand wildlife – who don't need the extra 'nudge' of persuasion that, say,

a townie might need before he or she picks up a toad. It is, in essence, a countryside diary, one which has greatly influenced my writing style and the structure of this Journal.

The Quiet Fields was one of my favourite books at school and then, when I needed it most, it helped me to rediscover my love of life, which led to the creation of the Priory. (There's a great message in the book about the finiteness of life, with BB considering his own mortality.) It's also an adventure. As BB said in his author's note, "My great hope is that the reader will accompany me on my rambles throughout the year... May he or she sense some of the delights I found in this still beautiful and wondrous world and perhaps feel with me a certain thankfulness to be alive". This is also the intention of *Fennel's Journal*. It is with BB's words in mind, and acknowledging the thirtieth anniversary of *The Quiet Fields*, that I dedicate this edition of the Journal to the book that inspired me and so many people to look a bit closer, and with more care, at the things around us.

What are the Quiet Fields? They are those undisturbed places set aside from intensive agriculture and the concrete sprawl of towns and cities. They are not polluted by the noise and emissions of motorways, nor suppressed by the manicured neatness of suburbia. They are wild places, quiet corners of the landscape left untouched, where Mother Nature is free to do her own thing. They are places in which you can observe wildlife and, by sitting quietly, find the time to look inwards, to find the answers to your questions. They're where our heartbeat slows to a more natural rhythm, where we can breathe, forget our troubles and, for a while, rejoice in being *properly* alive.

The countryside, with its vast horizons, fresh air and ever-changing seasons is, by its very nature, more life-giving and adventurous than any amount of modern indoor living. It inspires a love of natural history – everything from the birds that sing in the trees to the quality and richness of the soil beneath our feet. Most of all, it creates the desire to exist more naturally. And in doing so, we appreciate the balance of life. It is time to enjoy the Quiet Fields, and life itself.

I

THE CALL OF THE WILD

Think of a time in your life when you've faced a difficult situation. Maybe it was one of conflict, or grief, or something that threatened your health. Or it might just have been the dilemma we all faced when selecting sweets from the Pick 'n' Mix counter at Woolworths. How did the situation make you feel? What did you think? More importantly, how did you react? Did a survival mechanism kick in? 'Fight or flight' are well known, but what about denial, or the easy option of playing safe and opting for sherbet bonbons?

Each of us is likely to respond differently to the same situation, but an event that costs us greatly is likely to induce a dramatic response. Some events, and our reactions, will leave scars. But what if the situation costs us everything? What if it costs us our job, house, partner, sanity, and self-belief? And what if, on top of all this, it leaves us with debt that's equivalent to four times our annual salary? How then would we behave? Would there be enough swear words to describe how we feel? I know exactly what my response would be as this is what happened to me back in 2003. I responded predictably. I collapsed on the floor, sobbed without tears until my chest hurt and my eyes burned, and then sank into a state of emotionless non-existence, where life lost its appeal and the world was, for a time, without beauty.

I wrote about the incident, and how I recovered, in the first edition of Fennel's Journal. In it I made a promise to seek-out and spend time in quiet and safe places, where one can savour a gentle pace of life and a peaceful state of mind. The promise was fuelled by a commitment to not make the same mistakes again, nor allow myself to be corralled into an existence that lacked the true beauty of life. This promise became the foundation of the Priory, which is defined by the words "Stop – Unplug – Escape – Enjoy". It led to me share this Journal and, as of this year, launch a website to help champion the message. All this activity, *all this pleasurable effort*, has been my way of fulfilling the promise. But has it been enough for me to forget the ordeal of the past?

Five years have elapsed since I made the promise to pursue a better life. Has time been the healer it's reputed to be? It's been long enough for me to rebuild my life and repay most of the money I owe, but not long enough to forget the emptiness I felt back in 2003. That wound will never heal. And I'm glad that it won't, because it helps me to keep things grounded. While life now is infinitely better for me than it's ever been, I find that I've become hypersensitive to the pressures and politics of work. I have no time for the games people play to manipulate others into helping them achieve their aims. My doctor gave me a rational explanation for this, saying that my Coping Mechanism is broken and my adrenal gland is exhausted. A more brutal diagnosis would be that I'm a burnout, that my baseline stress is akin to the feeling one has when fingernails are scratched down a blackboard; that I'm a has-been, hobbling through life at a slower pace because I lack the resilience I had when I lived in the fast lane, when I worked 120 hours per week and survived on a diet of ignorance, caffeine tablets and lies. This brutal view isn't true, of course. I still find energy for things that matter. But there is another diagnosis: that as I grow older and wiser, I'm developing into being a lazy so-and-so. I'm easing up and reserving energy for activities that interest me. As H.G. Wells said in my favourite book, *The History of Mr Polly*, "He could not grasp what was wrong with him. He made enormous efforts to diagnose his case. Was he really just a 'lazy slacker' who ought to 'buck up?' He couldn't find it in him to believe it".

There are many parallels between my life and the fictional life of Mr Polly. As with Well's character, I often find myself looking inwards when I have "looked out of the window upon a world in which every possible congenial seemed either toiling in a situation or else looking for one with a gnawing and hopelessly preoccupying anxiety". In simple terms, I've been to the extremities of where selfishness and overwork will lead, and because of this I can see the flaw in modern life. As is said, we are "born to live, then worked to death". Sadly, when one has experienced something akin to a living death, one realises the importance of escaping the system and seeking out the things that have real meaning.

I don't mention any of this for sympathy, because

everything I've endured is of my own making (I chose my earlier life, and the responses that followed). I mention it because my story highlights the importance of the Quiet Fields. When one needs time out to recover from something, or to plan for and create something good, the quiet times and places become super-valuable. Anne Frank knew this when she wrote the words, "The best remedy for those who are afraid, lonely or unhappy is to go outside, somewhere where they can be quite alone with the heavens, nature and God. Because only then does one feel that all is as it should be and that God wishes to see people happy, amidst the simple beauty of nature. As long as this exists, and it certainly always will, I know that there will always be comfort for every sorrow, whatever the circumstances may be. And I firmly believe that nature brings solace in all troubles".

For many years I went fishing as a way of escaping my troubles. By casting a line into rivers and lakes I could savour the quiet corners of the landscape and study the wildlife around me. But then, last December, I fished for perch in a local pond. Sport was slow but the weather was fair. In a moment of enlightenment I reeled in, snipped the worm and hook from the line, and then cast out again, knowing that the float would remain motionless. *It had bobbed for the last time.* No longer was I distracted by the hunt for fish. Instead I was free to take in my surroundings, to wander away from the water and study things in detail. By removing the hook, I had begun 'fishing' for things other than fish. The countryman within me was reborn. My reason for being outdoors had changed. I felt the urge to listen harder, look more closely, and understand more about Nature. I needed to delve deeper, to explore the hidden places within our countryside that, once discovered, might reveal so much more about life. I needed to understand how to 'be' more natural.

While it's never possible to completely escape the stresses and pressures of the world, it is possible to keep the Quiet Fields in the forefront of our minds, so that when life gets too busy, too noisy and too troublesome, we can slip away from the battlefields and listen to the calming pulse of natural things. As Henry Thoreau wrote, "I believe that there is a subtle magnetism in Nature, which, if we unconsciously yield to it, will direct us aright".

Those who experience the Quiet Fields know that every second spent there is worth a thousand elsewhere. They make notes of every detail, capturing what they see, hear, and feel. While these experiences can be shared with friends, there's a temptation to draw the curtains to stop prying eyes scrutinising the 'resources' that exist away from the clasp of Man. Those who look in, in an emotionless way, don't understand the importance of these places. They're too busy looking, rather than seeing, as if what they seek is outside, rather than within. They haven't learned to tread carefully, and exist quietly.

To hear the 'quietness' of the Quiet Fields, one must first silence the noise within our minds. It's best to start before dawn, when the world of Man is sleeping.

JANUARY

II

FIRST LIGHT

*"We do not want merely to see beauty... we want
something else which can hardly be put into words – to be
united with the beauty we see, to pass into it, to receive it
into ourselves, to bathe in it, to become part of it. That is
why we have peopled air and earth and water with gods
and goddesses, and nymphs and elves."*

C.S. Lewis

"Country-folk rise early," said Alan, my farmer-landlord,
"so you'd better get some rest." His advice followed
news that I'd be manning the 2am lambing shift. My
startled expression told him that I'd rather be enjoying
a 'late one' in the pub. But Alan was a patient man and
knew that an eighteen-year-old didn't know any better.
By the following morning I was proud midwife to over
a dozen lambs and had completely forgotten about the
distractions of real ale. I'd learned that a night spent
lambing was, although exhausting, very rewarding. But
more than anything, I remembered Alan's words. He
taught me that country-folk do indeed rise early.

Those who work the land know what it's like to be
up and about while the majority of society is sleeping.

From the dairy farmer rising to milk the herd, to the poacher scrambling through woodland with a pheasant under his arm, each has witnessed the quiet world. These people have tiptoed downstairs so not to wake their sleeping families; they've lifted a latch on the door, and exited their homes. They've stood and gazed across silent fields and looked up at noiseless, star-filled skies. They know how differently the night air tastes and smells at different times of year (from the pure 'thinness' of winter air, to the rich and heady meads of summer), and they know how quickly the aches of yesterday disappear once a glow is seen upon the eastern horizon. Then there are those, in town and country, who choose to rise early for no reason other than for the sheer pleasure of it.

Today I woke at approximately 3.30am. I don't know the exact time, as I don't have an alarm clock. It was my internal clock that woke me. The same clock that tells me when I'm hungry and when I ought to go to bed, and the same one I blame whenever I'm late for something. Rising early is how and when I can 'find time' to do the things I love, when I enjoy a bit of 'me time' before the household awakens and responsibilities erupt from every angle.

At this time of year, 3.30am is several hours before sunrise. I could blame my body-clock for not adjusting to daylight-saving hours, but I won't. The reason I rise at the same time in winter as in summer is because I love this quiet time of day. It is when I can sit in silence, either in darkness or candlelight, and ask questions to my creative self. For this is the time when I do my best writing. The rational side of my brain has not yet woken (it likes an extended lie in, and then to be woken gently with thoughts of soft-boiled eggs and soldiers of toast), and so I'm free to explore a web of ideas that form in my mind. Sometimes, like today, I will sit downstairs with a cup of tea and scribble my thoughts onto a notepad. In the summer, I'm more likely to sit in the garden and let my thoughts build before I commit them to paper. I'll write down anything and everything that comes into my head, and then look for the links and angles between them. Mostly, however, I write about nature – both wildlife and human nature – and the lifestyle messages that come from a traditional and slow-paced rural life. While it's possible to gleam some ideas from reading about nature, the best and most detailed writing comes from actually being there and studying it first-hand. So, about an hour before sunrise, I leave my home and go for a walk along the lanes, fields and woods to witness the marvel that is an English dawn.

My walk this morning was brisker than normal. Stepping from my front door I slipped on ice and went skidding along the path like a drunken tap-dancer (hobnailed boots were never any good in winter). The sky was clear and a heavy frost was forming. I looked up, expecting to see a starry sky, but could see only a blur. So cold was the air that my eyes were watering and my breathing, which up until this point had been slow and steady, consisted of sharp intakes with longer and forced exhalations. (I'm not much good in cold weather.

My old gardener's knees and knuckles lock up and my bottom lip trembles. I attempt to act normally, but end up moving around like Joe 90. It's not good for my street cred. But in the dark, when there are not many folk about, I can get away with it. And if somebody stopped me and asked why I seemed to be doing an impersonation of a TV mannequin, then I'd say it had something to do with the moon. I'd then clomp away like an old-fashioned diver on the seabed.)

Soon I had left the slippy tarmac of suburbia and was walking along bare earth beside a river, and then across the grass of a water meadow (which 'crump-clumped' under my feet as the frozen blades gave way to my weight). Soon I was in Priory Wood, an oak wood that stretches along a ridge above the river valley.

Entering the wood, I noticed how the air had become slightly warmer and the ground softer. This should have been inviting, but it wasn't. My gladness to have escaped the frost was masked by the eeriness of the wood. There was no breeze to rustle the dead stems of nettle or bracken, no insects buzzing as in summer, no birdsong from the treetops, or a deer bounding across the woodland floor. All was so unnervingly, yet entrancingly, quiet; I was deafened by the noiseless scene. Do you hear?

Vincent van Gogh wrote "I often think that the night is more alive than the day". Not so in winter, especially in a wood at night. Everything this morning was silent. But it wasn't dead, merely sleeping. With the light increasing, I could see the subtle signs of life within the wood: the leaves of snowdrops and dog's mercury were inching up from the ground; the buds of honeysuckle and elder were swelling; mistletoe and holly were in berry and there was a muskiness to the leaf litter that I'd not smelled since autumn.

Some wildlife authors have been known to avoid writing about January because it is supposedly such a desolate time for nature. "There's not much happening, so why bother writing about it." But the joy of nature is in its detail. The subtle things I'd seen in the wood, even the silence I'd experienced, made this mid-winter moment so special. (Plus, on a different January day, one could fill a whole book with descriptions of frozen water – from hoar frost in the trees to cat ice in puddles.) There is always beauty to be found in any moment, if you look hard enough.

I stood listening for a while. There was every chance I'd hear the song of a mistle thrush, but I heard nothing. I continued walking through the trees, thinking all the time about the birdlife that would abound later in the day. Lapwings and golden plover were already in the fields; finches, tits and nuthatches would be seen in the wood; robins would be heard defending their territories; jays, magpies and rooks would be in the treetops; mallards, moorhens and coots would be on the river; and at the end of the day, a thousand starlings would be flocking home to roost. But alas, there would be no dawn chorus. For as in the hymn, "in the bleak midwinter, frosty wind made moan".

An oak tree marked my regular exit from the wood. Part clothed in ivy, contorted by its search for light, and silhouetted against the pale blue sky, it encouraged me to stop, look up and gaze around. I saw a faint amber glow appearing on the horizon. Night was becoming day. It reminded me of the gift, from parent to child, that instilled my love of nature. It was when, as a young boy, I was woken at first light by the sound of curtains being opened and my mother saying, "Fennel, wake up. It's going to be a beautiful day."

III

SILENT WHITE

"Sunshine is delicious, rain is refreshing, wind braces us up, and snow is exhilarating; there is really no such thing as bad weather, only different kinds of good weather."

John Ruskin

The promise of a beautiful January day was fulfilled. The morning was crisp and clear and then, in the afternoon, a south-westerly brought with it early spring temperatures that urged me outdoors. The weather remained fine for several days and then, after initial concerns about such a dry winter, we had more rain than the rivers and culverts could handle. The ground became claggy and I felt sorry for any livestock left out in the fields. But then, last week, a cold snap brought with it a flurry of snow. Nothing serious – just three inches or so – and definitely not a 'blackthorn winter', but it was enough for Mrs H and me to make a snowman in our garden. (We called him Wurzel, and welcomed him into the world by saying "Ay mate, can you smell carrot?") The local children enjoyed some early-morning sledging, but before anyone could get carried away and shout "snowball fight!" the news reporters began dampening our spirits with headlines such as: "Traffic Chaos Hits Britain," "Holidaymakers Stranded," "Water-mains Ruptured," "Salt Shortage Threatens the Nation," and, best of all, "Goat Decapitated by Speeding Sledge". Okay, so I made the last one up, but you get the picture. The snow had barely settled before people were wishing for it to thaw. But it was premature doom anyway. Before the gloom-bringers could decry that "Snowmen are the Coal-munching Sentinels of Satan", the snow began to thaw and sledges scuffed to a halt. By lunchtime the snow was little more than brown sludge upon the roads and by teatime it was just the memory of a sobbing child.

I wondered whether a person's lasting memory of the snow would be of excitement and adventure, or misery and chaos? If you took the journalists' words for it, then the day it snowed was one to forget quicker than snowmelt dribbles down a gutter. But for me and many of my friends, it was a day to remember, for all the right reasons. I'll tell you why in a minute, but first let's consider what might happen in the future, when historians flick through the news archives. I reckon they'll conclude that the "Great Snowfall of 2011" caused everyone to have a terrible time. All because journalists know that bad news sells and because, whether we like it or not, it gets our attention. We have an appetite to see and hear others suffer. We might sympathise and wish them well, make charitable donations and talk with empathy over coffee, or we might mock the afflicted. But do we really want to hear such bad news? What about the good things that happen to others? Would it only make

us jealous, or would we, as a society, feel inspired and energised by good news?

Douglas Adams wrote that nothing travels faster than the speed of light, with the possible exception of bad news. And, while we're in the fictional vein, Terry Pratchett wrote that no matter how fast light travels, it finds that the darkness has always got there first. But blaming Nature for our problems? That seems all too easy. People who do this are unable to accommodate the changing seasons; they prefer to be a green leaf on a bare branch. But for every person who attempts to be a dormouse in ice-skates, there is another who wraps up warm and stays snug at home. However, this doesn't make compelling news. "Snow Brings Joy to Millions" isn't going to headline when Arnold Scrudgebottom and family are whingeing about waiting an extra hour in the departure lounge.

I accept that the majority of society would rather hear about horrid, sad, depressing, draining, agonising and life-sucking misfortunes, especially when brought about by Nature. (The same entity that once had the nerve to call itself 'Mother', but which appears to have disowned its disobedient child.) Or is it that we have cut all ties with Nature in an attempt to fly the nest and defend a territory of our own? A brick-built, concrete-paved, super-nest where we attempt to play God and be masters of our own kingdom; where streetlamps blur the distinction between day and night, and where a treeless skyline makes it difficult to determine the time of year. This is not the world of the Priory, nor is it the way that my friends and I seek to exist. We have a different calling, that leads us to places, and states of mind, where we can exist more naturally.

Nature speaks to people in different ways. The recent snowfall proved this. Take my neighbours for example. There's a modern estate near to my home that houses all manner of folk. They're mostly commuters who, like me, prefer life away from the city. They seek the benefit of fresh air and, in return, spend four hours a day reading books on the train. There are downsizers, too, and a handful of elderly residents who've seen the benefit of living close to the shops. I've given each of them names, but admit to not knowing them personally. I noticed all manner of behaviours as they woke and saw the layer of snow. Slapdash Sid, the one with Clingfilm double glazing, had made a makeshift snow shovel from a plank of wood and a piece of rigid cardboard. It was working okay when I passed him, but when I returned he was cursing its sogginess and flaccidity. Which made me think of Takeaway Tony, the local couch potato. Tony was likely only concerned about whether Young Phil, the moped-riding pizza delivery boy, would be able to deliver his 11am Deep Pan Hawaiian. Then there was Centrally Heated Henry, who was standing on his doorstep wearing flip-flops, shorts and a T-Shirt. He was pointing at the snow as if mocking its inability to influence his Saharan microclimate. Pinstripe Phil had jumped into his company car and literally spun off down the road. His flashy motor was abandoned at the first incline on the estate. Then there were people I couldn't see. Meticulous Minnie was no doubt in her kitchen writing another letter to the council, highlighting how the snow had once again demonstrated their ineptitude at providing adequate facilities for the local vegan community. Facebook Fanny was probably updating her 'wall' with the comment, "Snow. Woe!!" But then there was 'Great Aunt' Winnie, the one resident to whom I speak daily. Now in her eighties, she was the person most like to be affected by weather. Was she warm enough? Did she have enough food in the house? Was she happy to see the snow, or was she worried by it? She wasn't at the window when I arrived at her house. She didn't answer the door. My heart sank, then quickened. I decided to check the back door, but as I entered through the side gate I could see that she was in the garden, topping up her bird feeders. She at least

knew the importance of food to wildlife in conditions such as this. Clearly, there are those who adapt to the weather, and those who cannot. Then there are those special people, like Winnie, who are attuned to the needs of wildlife.

Let us set the record straight, in case historians of the future seek an alternative view of the fateful events of "Winter, 2011". Let us tell them this: the snow was fabulous. Its falling beckoned us outdoors. We had to squint, such was its brilliance. We watched how it settled upon branches and chimney-pots, and drifted against walls and shrubs; we studied the tracks of blackbirds and robins across the lawn; we listened to how it calmed the distant roar of motorcars; and we felt how it made the air seem, somehow, warmer. We were compelled to stand still in the garden, just breathing slowly and smiling ever so gently, while waiting excitedly for nothing to happen.

Of course, there's always something going on. But compared to the fast-paced frenzy of the human world, a quiet moment standing amongst the snow was pure heaven. It was sensory overload in silent form. It asked us to stop for a while and take stock. It was the magic of the Quiet Fields cast upon us.

Later that day, after I'd finished laughing about Slapdash Sid's attempt to clear his drive, I walked across the meadow and up into Priory Wood. I knew that the badgers in Ruskin Sett would be having their cubs and that the bats in the hollow oak would be thinking about stretching their wings. The snow might have calmed the landscape, but there was plenty going on underneath. Sure enough, when I got to the wood, I could see snowdrop and coltsfoot flowers nodding above the snow and spikes of dog's mercury pushing up through the winter blanket. On the edges of the wood, clumps of nettles made the snow settle in mounds and above them, the ebony buds of ash contrasted the winter backdrop. Up in the trees, finches and marsh tits were chattering, and rooks were standing in their nests, arranging twigs and cackling as they prepared for their spring clean. But the highlight for me was exiting the wood and hearing the first skylark of the year.

There was so much life above and below this layer of silent white.

MARCH

IV

SIGNS OF SPRING, FROM WITHIN

This morning I decided to sit in my garden and catch a few rays of early spring sunshine. At first, I questioned why I chose to be outdoors when I could have been in my study enjoying the comfort of central-heating and the draft-free delights of double-glazing. But seeing the sun disperse the morning mist and then, at around ten o-clock, hearing a blackbird herald the joys of spring, I concluded that my home was too warm, too stuffy, and with not enough fresh air to inspire me to do anything indoors. I needed to be outside and feel the breeze, feel sunshine upon my bleachy-white post-winter skin, and feel alive.

I opened the door to my garden and felt the cool but brisk morning air. I straightened my back and took a deep breath. The air was cool and fresh, but, somewhat disappointingly, was scented with a mixture of countryside and town. (A typical sensation from a north-westerly breeze that brings with it the wildness of Greenland, the freedom of the Lake District and the whiff of Abdul's Kebab Van up the road.) No matter. It was spring air. The sort of air that enters our lungs, takes a look around, and clears out the cobwebs. The same air that makes us cough with shame when we feel the tightness of our lungs against the cold. "Okay," we say, "so we've been cooped up for too long, but we're here now. Let's forget all those evenings spent in front of the TV, and work on a plan to be outdoors as often as possible." This is how I greeted the spring air this morning. I then rubbed my eyes, brushed the dust from my clothes and stepped forward into a spring garden.

The sun was relatively low on the horizon and lacked its summer intensity, but its rays felt mildly warm. If I closed my eyes, I could imagine the long and relaxing days of summer. But when I opened them, and looked at the mug of tea in my hand, I could see steam rising into the cool March air. I was immediately reminded of the heavy dew and misty start to the day, and the cold night that preceded it. March has the ability to lure us outdoors, and then promptly remind us of the benefit of woolly undies.

I walked in slippers from the back door to my garden shed, opening the shed door and immediately catching a waft of hibernating mice (which smells like stale urine, pine nuts and moss. Or, as Mrs H describes it, "like a Yeti's scrotum"). I reached for my gardening boots, which were on a shelf in the shed. Phew. No mice in there, though the boots were cold and rigid. I put them on my feet, laced them up, and then walked a few paces to loosen their winter stiffness. My waxed waistcoat, which was hanging on the back of the shed door, was white with mildew. Its pockets were bulging with something unfamiliar. I checked them and found that they were full of wheat, a winter stash made by the mice. I left the waistcoat hanging, closed the door to the

shed and walked over to a seat in the garden that was, by this time, in full sunlight. And I've been here ever since.

It is now 11.37am. I know this to be the exact time because Mrs Stroppup, our neighbour but one, has started hoovering. Like she does at this time every day. She's one of those super-proud housewives who think that the world would be a better place without dirt, dust, pollen, grease, flies, ants and leaves. Indeed anything from outside that dares invade her home. (Heaven help a door-to-door salesmen...) She's a strange one. She rarely leaves the house. If she does, she wears an all-weather dressing gown and 'fearful' slippers. (They curl up at the front and squeak annoyingly, just like her mouth does when she speaks.) We neighbours feel sorry for Malcolm, her husband. He's a domestically oppressed man who seeks only a quiet life. Poor bloke. He was looking forward to his retirement and yet now he's a pensioner he gets nothing but day-to-day earache. "Malcolm, don't sit there!" "Malcolm, make yourself useful!" "Malcolm, those bins won't empty themselves!" And, most frequently, "Malcolm, how many times have I told you?!" His abuse is relentless. Malcolm's is the fate that every man dreads. If ever there was someone who needs the Quiet Fields it's him.

Ooh. Here we go. They're kicking off already.

"Malcolm! Look at these footprints. How am I supposed to hoover with dirt on the carpet?"

"Surry darleeeng. I onlee popp'd out fura newspeppa."

"It's not good enough! You know my rules. *No shoes in the house!* Now you either get on your knees and start scrubbing, or clear off into the garden. Just make sure you do one thing: *stop – bothering – me!*"

"I think I'll goo owt tooda gaardin. Thank y'dear. Love y'dear. Sorreeeee dear."

I can understand why Malcolm puts up with such abuse at home. He doesn't go out much because the older residents of the neighbourhood have never really accepted him. You see, Malcolm is not a 'proper' local. He wasn't born and bred in the area. He moved here when he was eight years old. Even though he's now in his late sixties, he doesn't benefit from any special treatment at the butchers ("wink-wink, I've added a few extra rashers for you"), and he has to step aside for those with muddier boots when standing in the queue at the Post Office. People frown if he sits on the prime-positioned bench on the village green (the one that's inscribed *"Scruffy Woof-Woof, May You Continue Your Barking in Heaven"*). But worst of all, he has to live with the shame of being turned down, for twenty-six years in succession, for a place on the Rusty Todgers Skittles Team (four-times winners of the Piddle & District Pub League). Sadly, the consequence is that Malcolm has to live a closeted and hen-pecked life. He hasn't the peace to savour a fine spring day such as this, or the social standing to be invited to Mrs Hefty-Curmudgeon's Spring Tea Party, which is happening this afternoon. (By not attending the party, Malcolm will escape the local gossip and won't be subjected to Arthur Peacock's moans about his 'understandable' inadequacies. Nor will he have to endure a face-full of Major Guffingdon-Trumps prize-winning onions. But alas, he will never experience Miss Thrice-Knightley's infamous sticky buns, or enjoy more than ten minutes away from 'she who wields the slipper'.) Also, I'm not sure whether the locals understand Malcolm's accent. He speaks like someone reading a phone directory while falling down an elevator shaft. From what I can deduce, his dialect is a cross between West Country, Liverpuddlian and Glaswegian. Which is odd given that he's spent most of his life living in the same street. Maybe he does it for effect? I don't know, but I do appreciate his upbeat greeting of "Mawnin Nebber, gownabeafynedae", when I know that his day will be far from fine.

Malcolm is now in his garden shed, rummaging about and making rattling and clanging noises as, I assume, he searches for something that's hidden beneath all manner

of clutter designed to keep his wife out of his private space. (The fences between our properties obscure my view of Malcolm, but I can guess what he's up to.) "Ahr. Thereyeare. Gotcha. Jurstwattaywureaftir."
Squeeeak. Clank. Scraaaawp. Clungk. BANG!
Oh, my. Sounds like he's finally lost it.
"Aya fewkern pilasheet!"
BANG! BANG-BANG!
"Dowyu getmessinwivme! Yougutwerktadoo!"
Brrrump. Brrrrrrumppp. BROOOOOOOUUUMMP!
Wow. Look at the size of that cloud of smoke.
Brrruuuummm.
Brrrruuuuuuummmmmm.
Bruuaaaaaawwwwwwmmmmm.
Aha. So that's what he's doing. He's mowing his lawn. That old petrol mower of his has never seen a squirt of oil. I'm amazed he got it going.
"Oooohyeeeaaa! Whoozadaddinowden? Thinkercud tekkit eezi diddya?"
Okay Malcolm, that's enough. I can tell you're enjoying the sudden rush of freedom. I think we'll leave you to it while we inhale the scent of that freshly cut grass. Ahh. Delicious. The first cut of the year, one of spring's finest moments.

As I sit here and listen to Malcolm enjoying his time outdoors, I am reminded that he and I are just as much a part of nature as the birds that have started singing and the leaves that are forming. (I heard the first chiff-chaff this week, and I'm sure that there will be willow warblers and yellow wagtails down by the river; there might even be a first brood of ducklings swimming along behind their mother. Catkins are flowering on the hazels and alders; pussy willows, kingcups, dandelions, daffodils and primroses brighten the landscape. In fact, other than the blackthorn flowers in the hedgerow, this March scene is speckled mostly with yellow.)

Malcolm and I were drawn to our gardens for different reasons, but we both feel happier and more alive by being outdoors. Like hedgehogs (that will now be waking from their hibernation) we feel our blood flowing strongly. We've got the energy of March hares and the inquisitiveness of badger cubs.

It's remarkable how winter quickly becomes spring, as if Nature decides that she has held her breath for long enough and exhales, breathing life back into the landscape. For there's definitely something in the air today. A gentle current. A sense of life returning. I can't determine whether it's something I can see, smell, hear or feel. Maybe it's a sixth sense. I don't know. The days are lengthening and the ground is getting warmer, and soon we'll have the fifteen hours of daylight needed for most plant species to flower. But what I sense is from within. I have become different, energised and inspired; not content to lie curled up in a hole, but instead to bound across fields with the joy of knowing that green buds are appearing, that dawns are accompanied by a chorus of birdsong, and the landscape is showing the signs of spring.

APRIL

V

BIRDSONG

"The bird upon the tree utters the meaning of the wind
— a voice of the grass and wild flower, words of the green
leaf; they speak through that slender tone."

Richard Jefferies

A world without birds would be a sorry place. There'd be no dawn chorus to wake us, and no feathered friends to eat our leftover chips when we're in the park. Spring in the countryside would be eerily quiet and our town parks would begin stinking of vinegar and grease. Wherever you live, it wouldn't be good.

A recent report by the Department for Environment, Food and Rural Affairs (Defra) provides sobering statistics about the state of the breeding bird population in the UK. If you'll bear with me, I'll share some of these figures with you.

The Defra report provides trends in bird populations between 1970 and 2010. It shows that the overall population of breeding birds in the UK has remained constant during this time. However, this is skewed by a 30% increase in seabirds. Woodland and farmland birds are in serious decline. Their numbers dropped dramatically during the '80s and '90s and have struggled to recover. There are only half as many farmland birds today as there were in 1970, and woodland birds are down by 19%.

The statistics include some worrying trends. For farmland birds: grey partridge, turtle dove and corn bunting have declined by over 90% and yellow wagtails have declined by over 70%. (The turtle dove population has halved within the past six years.) The good news, however, it that stock doves, goldfinches, woodpigeons and jackdaws have more than doubled in number. For woodland birds: wood warbler, willow tit, tree pipit, spotted flycatcher, nightingale, lesser redpoll and capercaillie have declined by over 70%. (Willow tits have declined by 43% in the past five years.) House sparrows are down 68% and blue tits, tawny owls, wrens and chaffinches are also in decline, but by less than 10%. However, blackcap, great spotted woodpecker, long tailed tits, green woodpecker, nuthatch and sparrowhawk have doubled their numbers.

The Defra report cites the cause of the declining number of farmland birds as "land management changes and intensification of farming that took place over a long period, such as the loss of mixed farming, a move from spring to autumn sowing of arable crops, change in grassland management (e.g. a switch from hay to silage), increased pesticide and fertiliser use, and the removal of non-cropped features, such as hedgerows. These changes resulted in habitat loss, a lack of suitable nesting habitat, and a reduction in available food sources." Reasons for the decline in woodland birds are quoted as "changes in woodland structure through ageing, a decline in active woodland management, and past poor woodland conservation, resulting in a lack of diversity in habitats and food sources in the woodland environment; [and] loss of habitats and food sources through damage caused by increasing deer populations."

It doesn't get much worse than this, does it? I could quote all the published stats, but reading them would be too depressing. The simple truth is that there isn't enough food and breeding places for our birds. Our actions in the past have buggered up things in our present. (The statistics for insects are similar. The overall decline in butterflies and moths is greater than all other species, again due to habitat loss – especially over shading in woodlands.) Sadly, it seems that Rachel Carson's predictions in her book Silent Spring (published in 1962) are coming true.

It's common knowledge that birds are a good indicator of the health of our wildlife, because they sit high in the food chain. If bird numbers reduce then it's likely that something's happened to the food chain beneath them. If the habitats and food sources don't exist for insects, or if we wipe out the insects with pesticide, then birds will suffer. Ultimately the food chain could collapse. It's clear that land use is also a major contributing factor, but compared to other demands on the land (such as Government projections for an extra 85,000 houses per year until 2026) it's pretty clear where birds sit, if you'll excuse the pun, in the pecking order of priorities.

So what can we do to help? The wildlife charities and lobbyists are covering things at the macro level,

so membership of the RSPB or Wildlife Trusts would be a good idea, but addressing the micro level is also important. The required action is simply a case of 'being aware' of birds and taking an interest in them. If we have this, then it's a natural progression to do what we can at home – allowing our gardens to be a bit scruffier; putting up feeders and boxes, and not using pesticides; they all help. First we have to care, and then we have to act.

Is that all on the subject? Is that all I want to say? It is not. But it's as much as I can write at this time. First I have to believe, then I have to see for myself, and then I have to care. Care more. For things that matter.

What you've just read was written in St. James' Park, London. I'd just attended a meeting near to the Defra offices. As I passed the offices I called in to see an old friend, who handed me the report. It triggered my need to find somewhere green in which to sit, write, and recover. Although I was fascinated and horrified by the statistics of the report (a bit like getting the results of one's cholesterol test), I was embarrassed by how much I take birds for granted, and how little I knew of their plight. I returned home and checked my nature notebooks for the previous year. In an act of guilt, I share the bird records with you now:

January: rooks on old nests, but not yet building; shoveler, teal, gadwall, pochard, golden plover, lapwings and widgeon on the meadows; thrushes, finches, great tits, blue tits, jays, nuthatches, robins and magpies in the garden. Mistle thrush heard in the wood on 23rd of the month.

February: rooks now building; fieldfares and redwing on the farm fields; blackbirds singing strongly in the wood; first skylark heard; chaffinches and marsh tits in the willows by the river; owls hooting at dusk; jackdaws on the fields looking for slugs and worms; partridges now in pairs.

March: first chiff-chaff heard in the wood; divers gone from Cornbury lake; rooks building in earnest; moorhens building their nests on the river; willow warblers and wagtails by the withies.

April: swallows arrived 12th April, house martins arrived 18th April, cuckoo arrived 21st April; skylarks very vocal, defending their territories; blackcap and garden (?) warbler singing.

May: Priory Wood is alive with birdsong; blackbird first to sing at dawn, blackcap singing best; thrush last to sing at night; house martins building; swallows already nesting; cettis warblers at the Amwell; mayflies devoured on the wing by swifts (which arrived mid-May).

June: 'chizz-chizz' of fledgling cuckoos heard in Priory Wood; small flocks of fledgling starlings in the garden; swifts very active – saw a pair mate on the wing.

July: first brood of swallows have fledged; mistle thrushes gathering at dusk – a sure sign summer is on the wane; sparrowhawk very active in the garden, fledgling tits are easy prey; hobbies feeding on dragonflies by the river.

August: woodpigeons calling lazily at dusk; yellow hammer 'twitting' all afternoon; bullfinches on the thistles in the meadow; kestrels active over the fields (taking old shrews that are on their last legs?); chaffinches flocking; swallows on telegraph wires, whimbrel, redshank in flocks, readying for migration; chiff-chaffs' gone silent.

September: swallows and house martins gathering for migration back to Africa; robins have begun their autumn song (as the males and females fall out of love with each other); woodpigeons cooing "I love you Betty, I love you Betty"; swallows nesting again; lots of finches in the garden; skylark and chiff-chaff singing again (after silence last month).

October: willow warblers gathering by the river, readying to migrate; rooks and jays feeding on acorns in the wood; rooks flocking – rolling and tumbling – from late afternoon; woodcock seen on the water meadow; lots of birdsong in the wood – wren, goldfinch, linnet, chaffinch, multitude of tits, robin, song thrush, hedge sparrows; brambling have arrived.

November: lots more woodcock seen at dusk; grebes seem to have departed; resident mallards still active.

December: not much about. kestrels are fluttering; cock pheasants standing proud in the wood, young pheasants roosting in branches now; sparrows and female chaffinches in the garden; fieldfares on the hedges eating haws; partridges in large numbers in the fields.

So there they are. My bird notes for an entire year. Pretty weak I'd say; and not at all worthy of statistical scrutiny. There are some obvious omissions, like the green woodpecker that visits my lawn each morning in search of ants, the resident coots on the river, the buzzards above the meadow and the heron that visits my garden pond too often for its own good. And although I'd recorded the species and where I saw them, I had failed to record any numbers or the frequency of sightings. (This isn't surprising given that numbers affect me like water in a frying pan, but it highlights the importance of being both scientist and artist when it comes to studying wildlife. To be a naturalist, one needs to be a bit of both.)

Do birds sing louder now than they did in 1970? I couldn't tell you. I wasn't born then. But they've certainly got more to shout about today, such is their plight, so we need to listen a little harder to what they're telling us. I for one am rising earlier than usual, ahead of the dawn chorus, and, with these words, am doing my best to sing on their behalf.

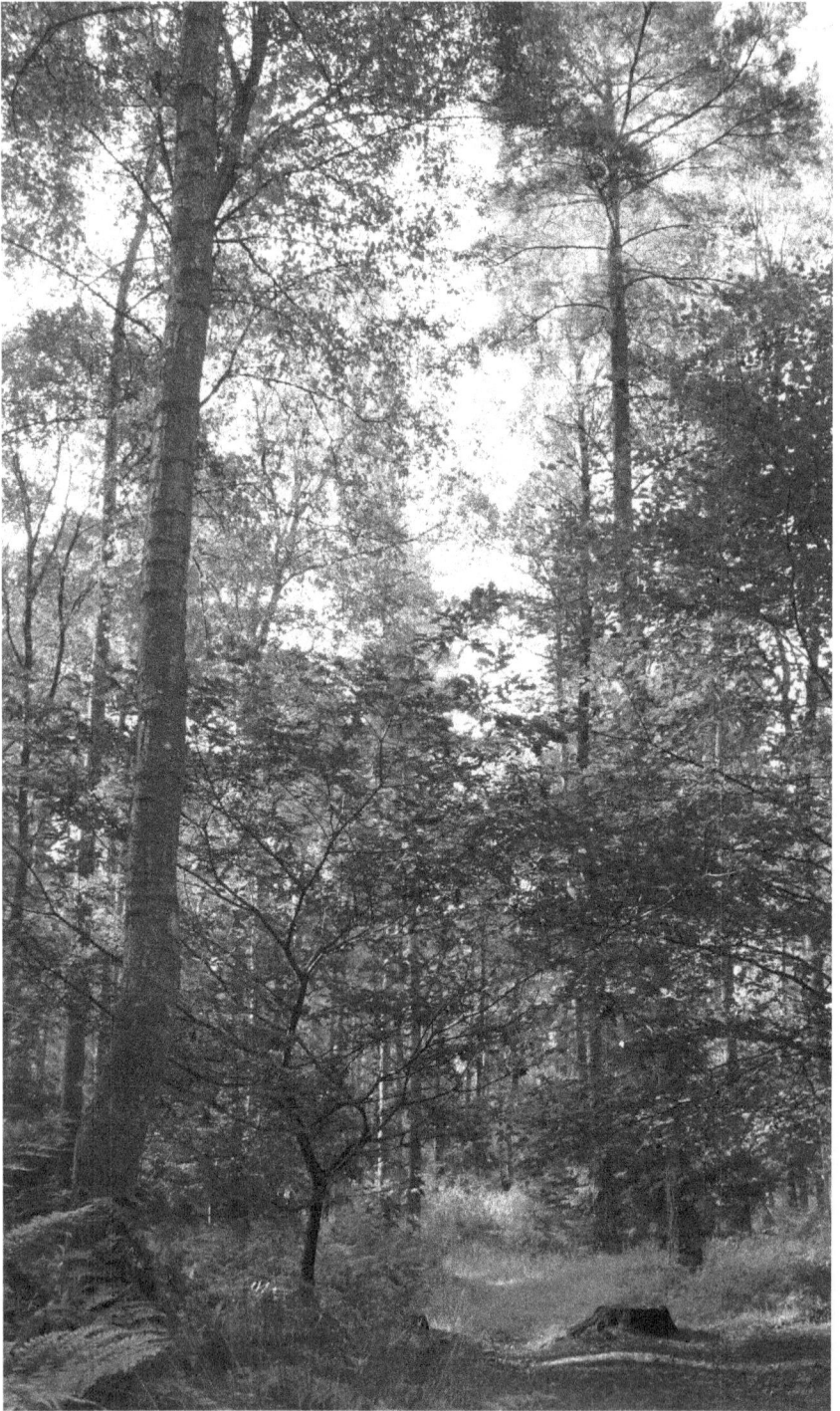

MAY

VI

THE COMPANY OF TREES

"One impulse from a vernal wood
May teach you more of man,
Of moral evil and of good,
Than all the sages can."

William Wordsworth

The British comedian Jasper Carrott once jested that Tree
Surgeons have the most pretentious job title in the world.
"They're blummin' gardeners," he joked. "What next?
Plumbers calling themselves U-Bend Gynaecologists?"
I can see his point. Watch a Tree Surgeon in action and
although you'll see plenty of skill and precision, there's
not a scalpel in sight. Instead, a chainsaw rips into limbs
that cannot flinch. (A tree cannot scream, and doesn't
feel pain like we do, but if it did, there'd definitely be
the need for 'Tree Anaesthetists'. Or, in plain English,
bigger earmuffs.)

I've never worked as a Tree Surgeon, although I've
felled and pruned plenty of trees. For 18 years I worked
as a gardener, and proudly so. There was no need for
pretension (except for three years post-graduation
when I called myself a 'landscape architect'). I shovelled

manure onto rose borders, got soaked when it rained and got chilblains and frostbite in winter. It was manual work. Poorly paid (in monetary terms) and the sort of occupation that kills conversation at dinner parties. But for all its associations with weed grubbing and dirty fingernails, I regard my time as a gardener as the happiest of my professional life. It was my vocation, my calling; an opportunity to spend every day in the fresh air, doing work that changed with the seasons, and being alone but for the company of plants.

The most valuable thing I learned during my time as a gardener (and my four years at horticultural college) was the importance of working in harmony with Nature. For example, if I was called to work on a new garden (or, for that matter, a municipal ground or large landscape) then the first thing I'd look at was what occurred there naturally. What soil type was there? What degree of drainage? What aspect to the sun and exposure to wind? But most importantly of all, what plant species were present? A garden next door will tell us what plants can be grown, but the trees, shrubs and herbaceous plants growing wild will tell us what should be grown. It's the wild plants of roadside, meadow and woodland that give us the best indication of what will grow naturally in an area. A skilled gardener or landscape designer will work with this to ensure that whatever plants they choose complement the natural flora. You just don't want things to die or look out of place. For consider how odd it would look to plant a pampas grass in the middle of a beech wood. You'd know straight away that someone had planted it. But if you randomly planted

some bluebell bulbs, then when they flowered you'd think that they'd been there all along. They would be at home in their environment. As Wordsworth wrote, "Come forth into the light of things, let nature be your teacher".

Most people cannot resist changing their environment to suit their own tastes. (Ever moved into a house and thought, "that wallpaper's got to go"? If you have, don't worry. It's human nature to seek to control things.) We seek to exert our presence and 'leave our mark' upon the world. Which is why we're the dominant species on the planet. But things fall over when we seek to work against Nature. Think of the vast plantations of pine trees that seep acid into the catchments of our upland rivers. These trees are not meant to be there, at least not as a monoculture. And then there are Rhododenron ponticum and sycamore trees, introduced to Britain as ornamental plants but which are now classed as invasive species. Through our ignorance, we've tipped the balance and are now suffering the consequence. But it's not all negative. Far from it. Organisations such as the Woodland Trust and the Forestry Commission exist to protect and manage our woodland heritage. They know the value of trees and how they benefit life, most especially our own.

Harmony between species can be easily observed in mature deciduous woodland. This is where you'll find the greatest diversity of plants, fungi and animals living together and where we can sit amongst something that's considerably older and bigger than us; where we can feel part of something beautiful. As Jane Austin wrote,

"To sit in the shade on a fine day and look upon verdure is the most perfect refreshment". I couldn't agree with her more. In fact, it's time for me to buy a T-Shirt printed with "Trees Give Me Wood!" and then go in search of some full-on tree hugging action.

It's now three hours and many bark-smooching moments later. I'm relaxing (in almost post-coital bliss) against the trunk of a beech tree at the edge of Priory Wood. It's a classic spring scene: a wood fringed by a meadow of flowering dandelions, buttercups, red clover, nettles, field poppies, comfrey, rye grass, fescue and ragged robin; the edges of the wood cascade with white May blossom and the yellow-green leaves of field maples; within the wood are flowering celandines, primroses, garlic mustard, arum, and a carpet of wild garlic. But it's the trees we're here to see.

In front of me are several beech trees, as you'd expect on the limestone escarpment of the Cotswolds. Their root systems are suited to the shallow chalky soil above the bedrock. But the wood is mostly made up of oak trees, so I assume the bedrock is fissured enough for the tap roots of the oaks to get a firm anchor. There are also ash and yew trees and, further towards the edge of the wood, hawthorn, field maple, silver birch, hazel and elder (although, technically speaking, elders are shrubs not trees). I've listed these trees individually to give you an idea of the diversity of the wood, but it's best not to view a wood as a collection of individual trees, rather a symbiosis of many organisms (so said Mr Bolt, my school biology teacher). A wood is a living thing. Both beneath and above the ground, and especially up in the

canopy where, at the moment, a dozen or more birds are singing. (Given the non-descriptive nature of last month's bird notes, I'll document that I can hear 'the flute-like whistle' of blackbirds, the 'careless rapture' of a song thrush, the spiralling and somewhat self-centred "chirichiri chereeep cheroo, finch!" of chaffinches, plus many other "scee-seees" and "chhrrrs" from great tits and blue tits.)

The casual observer might think that only the birds and I are talking. But they'd be wrong. Trees speak, too, and in many ways, the most obvious being the susurration of their leaves – which is a good indicator of the weather outside. (A woodland has its own microclimate – warm in winter and cool in summer.) But place your ear to the trunk of a tree on a windy day and you'll hear all sorts of clunking and groaning going on, rather like the noises within an old-fashioned windmill (the working type, not ones converted into holiday accommodation for amorous pensioners). I shouldn't jest. The trees in this wood are old and deserve respect. The beech and oak have been growing here for over two hundred years, and the yew is older still. Even the hazel, which has been coppiced over the centuries, could tell us how the locals responded to the Industrial Revolution. (Coppicing is evidence that a 'wild wood' is not as wild as we think, but has been managed or nurtured by man.)

Trees have seen so much change and yet keep on going, doing what they do and providing us with oxygen, while we mammals scurry about beneath them busying ourselves with things that are mostly nuts. The trees around us have not only seen much of history, they've played a part in it too, which is why they deserve our respect. Take oak trees for example. They are the most common and easily recognised trees in Britain. It's our National Emblem, too. We can thank the National Trust logo for that. Actually, no. I made that up. The person we should thank is King Charles II, who hid in an oak tree to escape his parliamentarian pursuers during the English Civil War. (The tree remains and is known as The Royal Oak, which has spurred countless pub names.) Thanks should also go to Admiral Lord Nelson, that fine leader of men who has, for the past 168 years, being standing on a column in London, waiting for a ladder. He's the man who lost the sight in his right eye at the Siege of Calvi in 1794 (as they say, he didn't see that coming) but, progressively bad jokes aside, he did foresee the future lack of English oak trees to make wooden warships (it took 6,000 oak trees – about fifty acres worth – to make one ship). In 1802 Nelson recommended to Parliament that oaks be planted in the Dean area of Gloucestershire (now the Forest of Dean). The rest, as they say, is history.

Yew trees are the most special of all. Regarded as being extraordinarily sacred by the Celts, and thought to symbolise death and resurrection by early Christians, they are often found in churchyards. Some were planted as a symbol of faith (and depending on your history teacher, to ward off evil spirits) but most of them actually pre-date the church that stands alongside them (the church being located at a pre-Christian sacred site). Yews are very slow growing (an inch or two per year) and can live for many thousands of years.

(The oldest yew in Britain – the Fortingall Yew – is estimated as being 2,000-4,000 years old). The ones in this wood, however, are mere youngsters, being only three hundred years old. But the real whippersnappers are the birch trees, which are barely thirty years old. Birch grows quickly and dies young. (The quicker the growth of a tree, and softer its wood, the easier it is for rot to set in; hence why the average lifetime of a birch is just fifty years.)

This isn't meant to be a history lesson, merely a statement of the character of this wood. And, given the tranquillity of this place, I now realise that I've done too much talking. Woods are meant to be quiet.

It is said that the very best relationships are those where friends can be together and not speak. Where they can enjoy 'comfortable silences' where nothing is uttered and yet each knows what the other is thinking. This is how it is in a wood, especially when we visit alone and have only the company of trees. After all, the joy of being alone, without feeling alone, is the great reward for being 'at one' with Nature.

VII

SPRING INTO SUMMER

Today, at first light, I walked my daily route eastward, towards the rising sun. My path followed the River Windrush, then across a meadow, and finally up into Priory Wood. In winter this journey culminates with me exiting the wood and watching the sun appear on the horizon. But today, when I stepped out from the trees, the sun was high and strong in its rays. It was 6am and the day had long-since begun.

Seeing the sunrise is the 'bright finale' of the walk. But the real pleasures are what I see along the way. This morning, my first observation was the 'sleeping' daisies in the lawn outside my house. Their white bracts were closed tight, keeping the pollen dry from the night-time dew. By the time I'd return home, they'd be open and basking in the sunshine. I tiptoed past them, acknowledging their need for a lie-in. They work so hard at cheering us through the day.

At the river, the marsh marigolds were still in flower. Reedmace and bulrush were spearing the water's edge, and a moorhen with three chicks (two less than last year, a sign of the reduced insect life) was dabbing across the water. The river was not its usual clear self. It had a murkiness that resembled very milky tea – more akin to its colour in March – which didn't bode well for any fishing plans I might have had later in the day. But the mists that were rolling and swirling across the water made up for the sulkiness of the water beneath.

Further along, in a slower part of the river, the first lily pads were visible on the surface of the water; their leaves having a dark crimson-purple colour (a sign of pigment concentration to help maximise photosynthesis), which will turn green on their upper sides as the leaves mature. Later in the year, the leaves will be upstaged by the lily's flowers – the largest of any wild plant in the UK. They are truly the 'swan among the flowers', as they are known in these parts.

The meadow was filled with waist-high buttercups and cow parsley. At its edge, two hares were grazing amongst meadow-grass and clover. They bolted when they saw me, disappearing into the foliage. The sea of yellow and white flowers rippled in the wake of these fine animals. Ultimately their disturbance was lost in the morning mist that lingered in the river valley.

With my mood lifted by the sight of the hares, and the 'weightless' elegance of the buttercups, I realised just how much this late spring had affected my daily pleasures. June is usually the month when the roadside verges reach their crescendo. When we're dazzled by the whites of May blossom and romanced by the pink elegance of dog roses. But this year the flowers have arrived late. For example, cowslips – nature's 'keys of heaven' – are in flower a month later than usual; and rapeseed – an iconic image of late April and May – is currently a mass of yellow in the farm fields.

(Its perfume is supposed to resemble warm honey drizzled over a digestive biscuit. But to me it smells, or rather stinks, like an old dog's blanket that's been left to fester. Not the sort of scent to encourage me to breathe deeply, or to run home and grab a Hobnob.)

Although British Summer Time officially began on the 31st March, it is not until the Summer Solstice on 21st June when we feel as though summer has properly arrived. The sun is highest in the sky, the day is longest, and the air is warm and scented with balsam. Swallows and swifts are dancing in the sky and flower-strewn hippies are dancing barefoot around Stonehenge. It is a time to rejoice, regardless of one's pagan persuasions.

For many country-folk, the first silage cut signals the traditional start of summer. Timed for when the cow parsley fades and the hogweed comes into flower, when the grass is tall and lush and has not yet been dried into hay by the sun. It's when the air is filled with the salad-like scents of mown meadows, and we begin thinking of picnics down by the river.

Today the dawn air was filled with heady watery scents, of water mint and marshes. At least until I entered the wood, when the air warmed and took on a peaty, compost-like smell of leaf litter and leather-like aroma of emerging ferns. But it was the sights of the wood that overwhelmed my senses. Not the green carpet of wild garlic that I was expecting, rather an ocean of bluebells – their flowers so vividly indigo-lilac, rather than a sun-bleached pale blue – protected from the sunlight by the canopy of beech leaves above. At least this late spring has given us something to cheer about: the best bluebell colour in thirty years.

I heard a blackbird call, and then a chaffinch. It was the chaffinch that called loudest, singing its little heart out, defending its pitch and calling to all the females nearby, saying, "Hey, ladies. Over here! Take a look. Aren't I stunning? I sure know how to make you frisk-eee!" But it was too early for all that stuff, and he was probably the only chaffinch awake in the wood. Soon the trees were alive with the chatter of blue tits and great tits. Robins, wrens, tree creepers, and a nuthatch followed; all singing against a backdrop of insects humming among the trees. Towards the edge of the wood, rooks and crows were crawking; their young having fledged the nests but still hounding their parents for pocket money.

And then, as I exited the wood and walked into a field of barley, I heard the cuckoo. I knew it was here, as it arrived a while ago, on the 25th May – the same day that the mayflies began fluttering from the river. (I say 'it' because, as we all know, there is only-ever one cuckoo. And it sings only for us.) But my excitement for the cuckoo was soon replaced by amazement and disbelief as I heard it being out-sung by a nightjar. Both are visitors from Africa, but the nightjar's relentless call was boldest and most unusual. I'd only ever heard nightjars calling at dusk, but this one barely stopped for breath as it beat out its chirring, drumming, call. It had a haunting eeriness, affecting me like the sound of chains being dragged up a wooden staircase. (If you've not heard the call of a nightjar, then imagine recording the sound of a wooden-wheeled bicycle being ridden at speed across a mile-long cattle grid, and then playing it back through the speaker on a fax machine.)

I looked up, blindly hoping to spot the nightjar, but was distracted by the brightness of the sun high above the trees. I felt its heat upon my face and sympathised with the nettles next to me, which were already wilting. I saw dandelions in seed at my feet, and willows in seed along the woodland edge, each waiting for the wind to blow. But there was no wind, just the sun burning brightly in azure skies. I was witnessing a new season. Today would be a fine and hot summer's day.

JUNE

VIII

A SUMMER SUNSET

"To one who has been long in city pent,
'Tis very sweet to look into the fair
And open face of heaven, to breathe a prayer
Full in the smile of the blue firmament."

John Keats

Yesterday's walk was special, but today was not destined to be a red letter day, or a black letter day or a day of any letters at all. I would happily have torn the page from my diary. It began at 2am with a drive to the train station, and then a series of train journeys until I reached a city where people immediately go underground where they stand shoulder-to-shoulder and ignore each other. (Such is the anonymity of life in an ants' nest.) I then spent a day in a windowless meeting room arguing about numbers which, for some reason, got progressively smaller as the day continued. It was 7pm before someone set me free and 8pm before I ate anything. *So much for a healthy day at the office.* I slept on the train during my way home, at least until Oxford, when sunshine dazzling through the train's window woke me.

The scene outside was so different to the artificial

light that had strained my eyes all day. The western horizon was tinged in coppery hues and the sun was burning like sulphur and molten steel. The sight was like a thousand prayers being answered in one magnificent vision of amber, gold, magenta and violet. After a day of hard-fought negotiation, of fists banged on tables and chairs thrown across the room, the sunset spoke silently, conveying its message that the finest things in life are free.

I reached for my notebook and began scribbling all sorts of pretentious poetry about the beauty of nature and rural life, versus the ugliness of the urban world and a corporate life. But I couldn't capture the spectacle before me, or how I felt. The sunset was too majestic for words and my emotions were off the scale. And so I decided to do the obvious. I would get home as quickly

as possible, grab my camera, and then race to the highest hill where, with luck, I would be able to take a photo of the sunset before it was over.

That was thirty minutes ago. I'm now standing on top of the aforementioned hill, with a camera in my hand and a sun burning like a magnesium flame upon the horizon. I've taken the photo and, in doing so, know that the day was not without meaning. If nothing else, I have the joy of knowing that I'll be able to share the vision with you.

Tomorrow the sky will be reborn, bathed in the brilliance of a new sun. But for now, the sunset is here. And here am I, scribbling these words as fast as I can while not taking my gaze from the horizon. But the words are worthless. At times like this, you have to lift your head from the page and see it for yourself.

IX

HEAVEN'S ABOVE!

Mrs H and I have purchased a telescope. There are two reasons for this. Firstly, because my beloved has taken an interest in stargazing, and secondly because I've taken an interest in the au pair who's moved into the big house across the street. *(Jeepers. What a constellation! That must be Triangulum australe, the Southern Triangle. I must have accidentally strayed into the 'Southern Hemisphere'.)* Unfortunately for me, Mrs H has decided to position her observatory (a deckchair) in the back garden. So my hopes for a sneaky gawp at Sexy Selene have been dashed, and all attentions are aimed at the night sky. This is for the best. I shouldn't have been distracted, and if I'd got caught peeking then I would have ended up seeing stars anyway. So I'm going to grab a chair and join my other half in the garden to 'see what I can see'.

Right. I'm in the garden now, sitting next to Mrs H who is staring through the telescope at the night sky. The time by the hands of Mrs H's observatory watch is, so I am told, "A little after midnight, somewhere between 12.07am and sunrise, maybe 'about two', or 'before three', but don't ask me such stupid questions when it's dark and I don't have a torch". I should have known better than to ask her while she was engrossed in her stargazing. However, this new hobby of hers requires further discussion.

"So what you looking at?" I enquire.

"Stars," replies Mrs H.

"I know that. But which ones?"

"The ones up there."

"Aren't you supposed to know their names?"

"I do know. They're stars."

"I see."

"Yup. But they look bigger to me."

"I know. You're the one with the telescope. But you should be more informed. I bought you that book, remember?"

"Yeah. The one that bored me silly with all that astrobabble about parsecs, mizars, miras, cephids and globular clusters."

"Oh, I remember now. Wasn't there an entire chapter debating the benefits of a twelve-incher over a six-incher and how the wrong position can lead to blurred vision and a strained neck?"

"That's right. The chapter was entitled 'Refractor or Newtonian Reflector?' It confused the hell out of us until we saw that photo of a man holding a huge black telescope."

"Ah yes. We laughed for ages about that. So what type of telescope do we have?"

"Dunno. It didn't come with any information."

"Well, it may have done. But I 'might' have thrown it out with the packaging."

"Oh, right. Like the time you 'might possibly' have spilled red wine on our living room carpet?

Or the time you 'definitely didn't' leave a fountain pen in the pocket of your shirt when you put it in the washing machine with my work clothes?"

"Maybe. But that was ages ago. We're over that now."

"So you are."

"I get the message. I'll take this as my cue to shut up and let you carry on doing what you're doing."

"Good call."

Blimey. Mrs H is taking this astronomy thing seriously. Or maybe she thinks that Friday's "because I love you" present of a rug for the living room floor had something to do with me wanting to conceal a four-foot blotch of red wine? One can never be sure. These women are curious creatures. I'd best support Mrs H by staying with her out here in the cold while saying nothing and making sure that this pen (which is fabulously clean after its accidental wash) doesn't make too much noise as it scratches along my notebook.

Actually, I'm really pleased for Mrs H. She's wanted to take up astronomy for years, so it's nice to see her indulging her hobby. One day we hope to live in a place remote enough to escape light pollution. Then she'll see a million more stars and enjoy her hobby even more. It's all part of our dream of living a quiet rural life. For now though, she's content to look and wonder. She doesn't need to know about nebulae, astronomical units or the Antoniadi Scale; it's the mystery of space that fascinates her. By 'staring' at the stars, Mrs H is able to lose herself in a place so far removed from the heavy pull of our own world. It's like the ultimate holiday brochure for the mind.

I have to admit to not knowing all that much about the night sky, which is embarrassing given the time I spend with my head in the clouds. I can identify the Moon, Venus and The Plough. And if I stare hard enough I can spot satellites moving across the sky and the residents of the International Space Station signing their guest book ("Great view, but the rooms are small and the food's crap"). But it's what I can't see that most intrigues me. What exists between the stars, there in the darkness? How many planets circle those distant suns? How many contain life? Is there anyone (anything?) out there writing about distant life, or how the arrival of a blonde au pair made him or her drop a bottle of red wine on the living room carpet? Maybe there is. Maybe there's a parallel universe where everyone wears tweed, where nobody owns a microwave and the best job of all is being a postman who delivers only handwritten letters. Or maybe there's a load of little grey aliens wobbling about the galaxy in pudding bowls and sniffing their hands because, for some reason, their abnormally long index fingers smell of cow bum and Nevada hot dogs.

Thinking of aliens seems to have sent me all 'sci-fi'. I hope Mrs H doesn't think I'm mocking her hobby. But it does invite one's imagination to run wild. Also, I like the thought of places where anything's possible and 'Earthly' laws can be bent to suit one's plot. *"Space, the final frontier, where man boldly splits his infinitives and where nobody can hear you scream (or, it seems, when you zip up a spacesuit while singing about a lucky star); where wearing a red stretchy top will seriously reduce your life expectancy, and employing a robot called Hector is a bad idea if you're thinking of moving to one of Saturn's moons; it's where aliens have evolved to burst through your chest but haven't learned how to blow their nose, and where warp speed is somewhere between 'can't take any more' and 'really can't take any more'; and, finally, if you don't do as you're told, your dad turns your best mate into a pile of clothes and then chops off your hand with a light sabre. It's enough to make you jump to light speed and whizz about in Hyperspace."*

One sci-fi quote that's especially relevant to our understanding of the night sky is "A long time ago, in a galaxy far, far away". When we look up at the stars, what we're seeing is light that's travelled millions of light years (our own galaxy is 100,000 million light years across). Given that light travels at 186,000 miles per second, we can appreciate the distance the light has travelled, and the time it's taken to reach us. So when we gaze at a star, what we're seeing is light that was emitted tens of thousands of years ago. In some instances, the star may no longer exist, even though we're still receiving the light from it. It is a way of directly looking at, if not into, the past. Such is the timeless beauty of space.

Postscript:
Given the tilt of the Earth, we don't really "look up" at the heavens unless we're at or near the North Pole. Here in the UK we're actually looking across to them (when we're standing up, we're nearly horizontal). It's good enough reason for us to raise our eyebrows, reach for a beer, and say "Heavens above!"

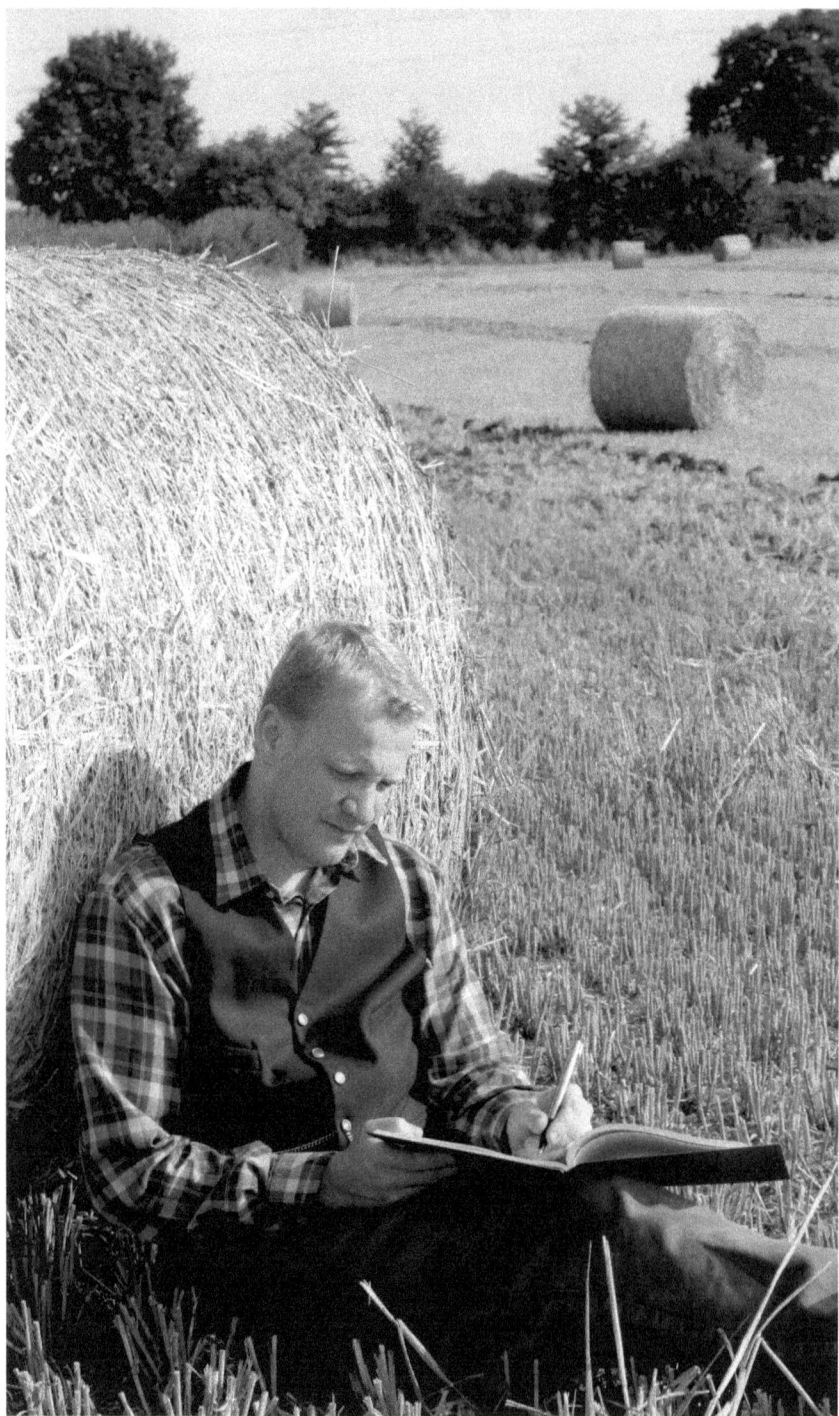

X

THE LAZY DAYS OF SUMMER

"August is the happiest and busiest of all the months, and heaven's rich reward of industry and patience; now are the almost deserted barns opening wide their doors, waiting the treasures of the field."

Clare Read

It is the end of August. The harvest is complete. The combines that worked the fields through day and night have departed; their dust and rattle have gone and the landscape has recovered its tranquillity. I am making the most of this quiet time by sitting against a bale of straw, gazing across the stubble at a flock of pigeons that are gorging themselves on the wheat left by the mechanical harvester. The farmer won't deny them their summer treat. No shotgun or bird-scarer sounds. The air is quiet save for the twitting of swallows overhead; there is no breeze to rustle the trees or hedgerow, and no insects buzzing nearby. I sit here in contentment, with notebook upon my lap and the heat of the sun warming my face.

How nice it is to spend time alone, motionlessly, just watching and listening, and reflecting upon the thoughts that enter one's mind. I feel safe here, far away from the roar of motorcars, the clatter of trains and tapping of fingers on watches (where a pat on the back is only ever a 'foot' away from a kick up the backside). Here I can slump onto the soil and rest. I could lie down to sleep, or look up at the blue sky and think about the world around me. I'm going to take the second option.

I'm not really alone, as you are here with me. I can trust you to remain quiet (though my pen is making an awkward scratching noise, as if it's telling me you'd rather be here in person rather than in spirit. Imagination will have to suffice for now). Lay a coat on the ground and put your feet up against the bale of straw. It's rather comfortable; though I'm sure you'll get 'pins and needles' in your legs if you lie with your feet up for too long. No matter. The day is fine. The ground is warm and it seems the right thing to do. A lazy moment for just you and I.

Sitting or lying still, for the length of time it takes to imagine an eagle in flight (which can either be seconds or hours, depending upon how long you watch it soar), is enough to stir one's soul. We can relax our muscles and, in feeling the lack of tension, tell ourselves that we deserve this moment; that we're owed a few seconds where the world leaves us alone and time is ours; where we can close our eyes without the urge to sleep. If someone could see us like this, they'd know that the best smiles come from lips at rest. But alas, peaceful rest is frowned upon in the world of 'work and bills and energy pills'. Putting one's feet up, or having 'forty winks', or daydreaming while gazing out of a window,

are the behaviours of a slacker, or so we're told. If you want to get on in life, you have to keep going, keep toiling, until the centrifuge stops or a clock 'hands' you a ticket to freedom. With luck, you'll still have the energy to sleep. Fortunately for us, these rules do not apply to the Quiet Fields. Here, there's no end-of-year Performance Dialogue or Personal Development Plan. No aspirations, goals, drivers, motivations, carrots, rockets, boots, bonuses or written warnings. Just time. Alone. In quiet surroundings. Where a man can sit motionlessly and feel life returning to his veins.

I mention the contrast between work and recreation (and self-flogging versus self-recuperation) because I'm sitting here for a reason. I should be at work, but things didn't go to plan this morning. I had one of those defining meetings that start with

"We've been considering you for the job," and end with "…but upon reflection we've concluded that you're not the person we're looking for". And so I decided to take some time out to sit and reflect upon the playground games that had brought me here.

The interview had gone well, and we'd got talking about the 'package' involved. The interviewer asked what it would take to get me to work another fifty hours per week. "Obviously we couldn't pay you double the money for double the time, so how about we look at giving you a senior-sounding job title and the opportunity to deputise for your manager?" Hmm. The offer reminded me of the Thoreau quote "The price of anything is the amount of life you exchange for it" and the words of William Henry Davies, "What is this life if, full of care, we have no time to stand and stare".

"A hundred hours per week," I replied, "would need to be spread over seven days, but after time spent commuting, would leave me only six hours per day in which to eat, sleep, see my family and attempt to have a life. It sounds a bit one-sided. How about you give me six months off per year?" The interview panel looked at me and laughed, as if I was the only one to have made an unreasonable demand. I shook my head, and then shook their hands goodbye. I left, glad to have remained a wealthy man, rich with time, even if it had 'cost' me a promotion and an alternative future.

Thomas Hardy wrote that "Time changes everything except something within us which is always surprised by change". I think this is why I'm sitting in this field, feeling none-too-pleased with the busy world of

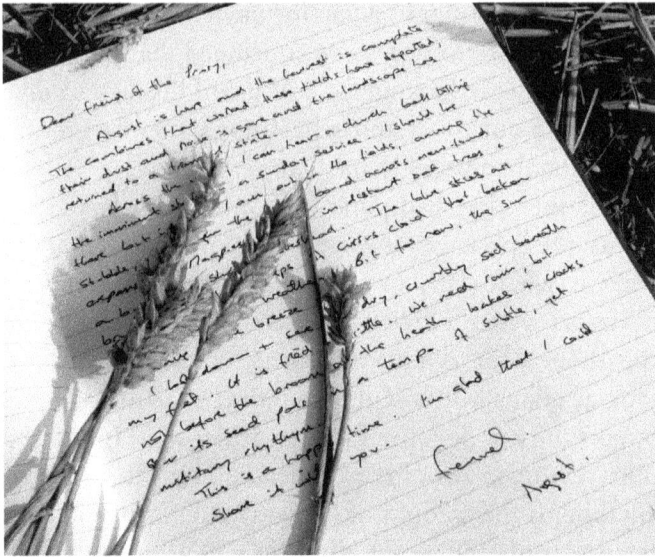

work and disheartened by people's belief that being productive somehow involves being restless. I am a traditionalist, and I don't warm to change as quickly as others. I like things to be as they've always been, unless an improvement comes along that builds upon and acknowledges the traditions of the past, thereby inheriting its character. To have been 'the person they were looking for' would have required me to ditch all my values and become someone I'm not. It was too great a sacrifice. So here I sit, career-limited but rather smug that I've remained in control of my life and true to the promise I made all those years ago. As Richard Jefferies wrote, "The hours when the mind is absorbed by beauty are the only hours when we really live, so that the longer we can stay among these things so much the more is snatched from inevitable Time."

So, while I have time, let us savour this August day. It is a day when not much else will happen. I'll continue sitting here until either the farmer arrives for the bales or the rays of sun become too hot. Later I'll walk home, checking, as I go, the ripeness of the blackberries and the fragrance of the wild hops in the hedgerows. I'll keep an eye open for the last of the Swifts, but I'm more likely to spot a bullfinch feeding on the thistles in the verges. If I'm lucky I might hear a yellowhammer, as they like hot summer days. But I doubt I'll hear the chiff-chaff for a week or two (they must get a dry throat in this heat, or go for a sing-a-long coach trip to Scarborough). Down at the river, trout will be rising to sedge flies. There might even be a hatch of flying ants to catch their attention. Who says that Nature sleeps on days such as this? Yet it is barely lunchtime. I know this because I can hear a church bell in the distance announcing the start of a wedding service. Someone's got fine weather for their Friday wedding. I could be there, supporting the happy couple or making a quiet prayer. But on a day like today, when I can sit amongst the stubble and savour the stillness and quietness of a summer's day, I know that this is the best place in which to appreciate God's work. It is all around me and, I feel, within me.

I look down, past this writing pad, and see dry soil amongst the stubble. It is fried and brittle. We need rain, but not before the broom on the heath bakes and cracks open its seedpods in subtle but military rhythm.

It is a happy time. I'm glad that I could share it with you.

SEPTEMBER

XI

THE AIR WE BREATHE

"Houses have but three functions: to keep us warm, dry and secure. Anything regarding character or location is incidental." So said a friend of mine as he and I viewed Number 12, Turnpike Avenue. It was to become the eighth property in his mortgage-free portfolio. *(Nice position to be in, eh? Mrs H and I are struggling to pay for one house, let alone eight.)* But I could never agree with his words, even though his properties were all buy-to-let. A house has to have soul for it to become a home, and for that, one has to love it.

I was reminded of my friend's words last night while watching a programme on television about house design. Mr and Mrs Designer Everything had no kids, no pets and no desire to acknowledge that they were over forty. They'd left the city and bought a greenfield site in the Cotswolds that overlooked miles upon miles of farm fields, woodlands and a river valley. I nearly dropped my stilton and crackers when I saw the location. It was the countryman's dream: an opportunity to live a rural life with no immediate neighbours, no light pollution and no traffic noise. The site was crying out for a Cotswold stone farmhouse. But what did they choose to build? A subterranean, concrete- and glass-walled 'bunker' with no carpets, no soft furnishings and no views. It looked like the reception lounge to an underground nuclear silo. But they liked it. And after much 'munching on my Jacob's' I concluded that it was they who had to live in it, not me. But what puzzled me was that this was a passive home. I'd never heard of such a thing before. At first, I thought it was somewhere a peace-loving vegetarian would talk nicely to a walnut before taking it outside and smashing its head in. But soon I learned that a passive home is an airtight building. It doesn't lose heat like a normal house, through offensive things like air vents, letterboxes, or windows that open. It is 'super-efficient', with the air inside being heated by sunlight which enters through vast curtainless windows. The air is then pumped around the house before being mixed with fresh air that's sucked in from outside. The stale air exits via a one-way pipe and the new air helps to freshen up the place a bit. *(Sounds rather restrictive. Whatever next? Clothing regulations? Airtight 'passive' underpants?)* The whole thing reminded me of my student days when, in an attempt to save money for beer, my four flatmates and I spent a month eating nothing but baked beans, tinned tuna and boiled cabbage. Passive? Pass out more like.

I accept that these soon-to-be troglodytes may have had planning restrictions forced upon their home ("Your proposed design is not in keeping with the rural aesthetic. We suggest you bury it") and that they may have found the transition from city to sticks a bit daunting, but what was the point of them living in the countryside if they had no desire to engage with it?

They should at least have wanted to look at it, even if they could never bring themselves to muddy their shoes. The Office of National Statistics reported last year that 250,000 people left London (replaced by 200,000 moving in), which tells us that many people are going in search of something different. If they were fortunate enough to move to a place where they could live without compromise, then why would they seek to live in ignorance of their surroundings? (This applies equally to someone in the city as in the country.) The house on the television last night was the 'passive' equivalent of an ostrich sticking its head underground (or, given the likely smell, sticking it somewhere equally dark but a bit more 'chewy'). I thought the whole point of moving to the country was to get fresh air and savour an outdoor existence? Sadly, modern lifestyles are luring us indoors.

These days we spend so long sitting in our centrally-heated houses and air-conditioned cars that it's easy for us to forget what it feels like to be outdoors. It would be all-too-simple to forget basic, natural, pleasures such as feeling a breeze on our face or looking up at a leaden sky and feeling the cool tickling of raindrops on our skin, or seeing water droplets form on our clothes when we walk in the mist, or feeling the crunch of snow under our feet, or, simplest of pleasures, lying amongst the daisies on a sunny day and watching clouds drift overhead. Instead, we (and especially the next generation) run the risk of becoming creatures of the shade: sad, grey-skinned beings with bulging unblinking eyes.

I'm passionate about quality of life, especially when seen in the context of the modern world which, when

viewed through the eyes of a traditionalist, has gone mad. Food is shipped halfway round the planet because people have forgotten the joys of seasonal produce; people (including me) work relentlessly to make ends meet; they become tired and reliant upon satellite instruction to guide them from A to B; children play virtual sports indoors rather than heading to green and life-giving fields; families watch wildlife programmes on television rather than venturing outdoors to discover things for themselves. They live blissfully in a cocoon of convenience, where everything is streamed, broadcast or delivered to their door. They don't need to open a window to get fresh air; they just spray an aerosol of 'Spring Meadows' around the room while waiting for the microwave to blitz a Calorific Pizza.

Of course, I have to include myself in this broad brush condemnation of modern life. I'll eat a pizza with the best of them and I tend to work longer hours than I should. (I've also been known to spend entire weekends watching *The Simpsons*.) But I have a promise to uphold, so I've got to take the high ground, even if I'm the person of whom I'm most critical. I think again of those city dwellers on television last night who became ground dwellers, all in an act of wanting to be free but, like a budgie in a cage, not knowing how to fly when the door was finally opened. Theirs is a classic example of the relationship between wildlife, the Quiet Fields, and Man. Many people like the thought of a quiet life, but lack the ability to slow down and catch their breath.

The Quiet Fields are not for everyone. They're not meant to be. If they were, they would no longer be quiet and we'd have to seek our escape in the deserted city streets. They call to some, but not others. Some people draw their energy from social events, but those who seek a quiet life need time away from people, among the plants and animals of a natural world.

'Being' outdoors requires us to do more than open the curtains. Many people push their faces to the window in an attempt to get closer, to see things more clearly; they don't realise that from the other side, their faces are contorted, pressed against smeared glass. They're too busy looking out, and not busy enough looking in. If they did, then they might find their way to unlatching the window or opening the door. And when they did, they'd realise that the door is not an exit, but an entrance. To the real world.

XII

...AND THEN IT RAINED

The sun rose late today. I think it's suffering from too many 'start of term' student parties. Waking for work felt like rising in the middle of the night. The roads hereabouts became gridlocked due to so many motorists 'leaving it until the last minute' before they left for work or did the school run. I am one of these drivers. I am supposedly on my way to the office, but have been sitting in my car for the past forty minutes wondering how travelling by car can be slower than using one's legs. I have travelled less than a mile. Still, this has been a good opportunity to people-watch. The view in my rear-view mirror is of a man shaving with an electric razor; a lady in the car in front is applying her makeup. I can see them clearly because they've got lights on inside their cars. Outside is still quite dark.

The dull conditions this morning (weather conditions, not traffic boredom) are made worse because it is raining. It's a cold autumn rain that falls steadily through windless air. It's heavier than a drizzle but not heavy enough to patter upon the roof of the car. The blades on my car's windscreen wipers are complaining, making a noise similar to a cow in labour. They think it's earlier than it is, whereas really it's almost

8am. I tell them that the clocks will be going back this weekend, which will give them an extra hour in bed. They groan as if saying "You're not the one shivering outside all night". I apologise and let them continue doing their thing, hoping that flinging their arms about will eventually get them warm.

Of course, as you would expect, I am far from worried about anything that delays the start of my working day. By the look of this traffic it will take me a couple of hours to travel the 40-odd miles to the office. Which, conveniently, is enough time to write this journal. So I'm sitting here with a notebook on my knee, capturing what I see and what I know is soon to come.

I'm 'travelling' along a road which runs alongside the River Windrush to where it meets its confluence with the Thames. All around are floodplains, willows and rushes, and further back are the woods that cling to ground that's more than ten feet above the water table. Through the car windows I can see the changing colours of autumn. The willows show the greatest range of colours: osiers are fully yellow, crack willows are orange-red, and goat willows are bronze-green. They're not yet shedding their leaves, unlike the poplars, birch and sycamore that are coating the road in a mottled quilt of yellow and burnt umber. The colours are matched in the hedgerows, where the hazel and field maples contrast the grey skies, but the hawthorn and blackthorn are still green. Even the elders retain their summer colour, although their tips have a tinge of purple. The oak and ash trees aren't yet turning, but the beech trees have leaves that will soon be falling to the ground. The roadside verges are spiked with the decaying, wet-looking stems of nettles and ragwort, and the sodden 'fluffy' flower-heads of willow herb and old man's beard. It looks like it's a good autumn for berries and nuts. There are acorns everywhere and even the ash trees seem to be sagging from the weight of their seed pods. Country lore says that a good crop of acorns beckons a hard winter, but I'll wait and see. In the meantime, I'm making a mental note of where the best sloes, elderberries, haws, rosehips and hazelnuts can be found. (The blackberries have already gone mushy and are no longer worth the bother.) Birdlife is more active than I'd expect in this weather. I can see a kestrel hovering alongside the hedgerow (it must be starving to be hunting in the wet) and a flock of finches just shot overhead. There's a sparrowhawk perching on a telegraph pole in front of me. He looks dark and sodden, none too pleased to be out in the rain or missing his breakfast television.

I'm rather pleased to be here, albeit in the comfort of my car. It's an opportunity to take a look around without getting a wet neck or a soggy notebook. Normally, car travel forces us to look forward, but today I'm moving so slowly that I can look all around. I can even take my eyes of the road to see what I'm writing.

Not everybody shares my pleasure. A young man wearing a grey suit has just exited his car and is walking, in obliviousness of the rain, along the line of cars, making gestures with his hands and shouting offensively. He's shaking his head and cursing at the drivers, as if it's everyone's fault that the traffic isn't moving. It seems he doesn't give a damn about the autumn scene around

him. Oh, no. He's bending over now, trying to be sick. Calm down, my friend. Calm down. Work to live, don't live to work. Your job should serve only to allow you to do the things you want to do. It's a facilitator, not Lord and Master. Focus on your breathing. Breathe slowly. Breathe slowly in, and slowly out. Soon the blood-flow to your brain will correct itself and you'll be thinking clearer and behaving normally. Then you'll be able to respond rationally to your situation.

We humans often 'give our best' at work and leave little energy for the more important things at home. We strive to succeed and better ourselves, but often run in the wrong direction, where we are swept up by the corporate jet stream.

Stress causes us to behave in a way that's opposite to our default personality. For example, a person who normally is patient and quiet will become abrupt and animated; an extrovert will become quiet and withdrawn. Stress is a hormone that's triggered in response to our environment, or rather our interpretation of that environment. It's a natural response. Fight or flight. Either way it puts us on edge. But it's not always healthy, especially for prolonged periods. Take that kestrel for example. It wouldn't normally be hunting in the rain. Its feathers will become waterlogged, which will make it progressively harder for the bird to fly and hunt. Its behaviour must be due to extreme hunger or to feed a late brood. And take the man in the suit (currently hunched over with his head in his hands). Clearly he needs to be somewhere urgently. I assumed earlier that he's a workaholic who can't cope with not being at work. But it's just as likely, looking at his behaviour, that he has an unforgiving boss who's going to give him a hard time for being late. Or maybe the man received a message telling him he must return home quickly because a loved one needed him. He's stuck in a terrible place, with his thoughts trapped in a body that's paralysed by stress. Bear with me while I go and console him.

Okay, I'm back. I was able to talk to the man, who told me his name was Craig. He wasn't in a good place, having lost his patience with the daily trudge to work. He told me that he'd been commuting to the city for the past three years but, because of the crowded trains, had recently taken to driving in. His shortcut to the motorway had become progressively congested and for the past month his journey had been taking him three hours. "I'm averaging twenty miles per hour," he told me, "and spending six hours a day in the car. Everything's so slow. I'm getting more and more tired. My patience is wearing thinner and thinner. I just can't see the point of it anymore." Craig was in no state to work, or drive, or do anything other than sleep. I encouraged him to go and sit back in his car, in the dry, and then pull over as soon as the road was wide enough to do so. His was a state that, sadly, I know too well. I've experienced it myself and have seen it in so many of my colleagues. We might jump to conclusions about our employer pushing us too hard, but in most instances it's the individual who's to blame for allowing his or her life to become imbalanced. Craig's employer hadn't told him to live sixty miles away. Craig had chosen to do so, and had suffered because of his choice. And because his levels of stress were so high, he was unable to see the positive side of his situation. He hadn't changed his focus to see the brighter side of the dull morning. Yet, when I spoke to him, I didn't ask if he was alright, merely if he'd seen the teasels next to him. He didn't know what I was talking about at first, until I showed him the prickly stems and seedheads in the roadside verge and explained how goldfinches love the seeds at this time of year. Maybe it was the distraction, or maybe it was getting him to think about something nice, but Craig's face softened and his eyes became brighter and bigger. He looked a changed man, all because of a humble teasel. As Vincent van Gogh said, "If you truly love Nature, you will find beauty everywhere".

There are occasions during the year – simple, beautiful moments – that induce a euphoric state. They're not complicated events, merely glimpses of something special that remind us of the natural beauty of the world. It is as if 'the moment' winks at us and we blush with embarrassment, flattered to have been deemed worthy of the invitation. Craig was privy to such a moment. As he walked back to his car he continued to shake his head, not in annoyance but at the daftness of his actions. His earlier frustration was because he wanted to be somewhere else. Now he wanted to be here. It's all about perception and appreciation. As Roger Miller once said, "Some people walk in the rain, others just get wet".

XIII

A WINTER FIRE

"Remember, remember, the 5th of November." Why? It's one of the best nights of the year, that's why. A proper burn-up in the garden, with sparklers, fireworks and a tray full of jacket potatoes. It's my sort of evening. Oh yes, and there's something about some dude trying to blow up the House of Lords. But that's an afterthought when presented with a *Sonic Skythunder* rocket that takes two people to carry it and has to be launched from a concrete bunker a hundred yards away. (Or, in most cases, pushed gently into the ground next to the patio and lit with crossed fingers.) Of course, I jest about the Guy Fawkes bit. Bonfire Night is a historic occasion that acknowledges the greatest conspirator in British history. No wonder we stuff old clothes with newspaper and make them into a life-size doll which we then throw onto the fire. Bonfire Night is traditional, that's the point of the message. Even if people forget the historic event of 1605, they shouldn't forget four hundred years of tradition that celebrates King James surviving the assassination attempt. It's a case of past meets present. One only has to look at the wood burning like a dragon's eye to see – quite literally – the life which once was, rising again. It dances like fireflies into the night.

The bonfire is a beacon to tradition, with each firework celebrating our heritage. But whenever I see the flames rise, I'm conscious of the break in the natural cycle of things. There's no slow decay of timber, instead a rapid release of energy that singes my eyebrows and turns my marshmallow-on-a-stick into a charred and delicious goo. What we're left with is a pile of ash, very sticky lips and the memory of good times.

I'm standing beside a bonfire at my in-laws, transfixed by the swirling yellows, reds, whites, blues and greens of the fire. Our Guy this year had fluorescent orange hair, purple trousers, a cowboy hat and Scooby Doo slippers. (We felt that historical accuracy was important for such a traditional event.) We painted an expression on his face that was supposed to say "Ooh, toasty" but ended up looking more like a toothless gurner saying "Cor, flowery baps!" Not at all appropriate for a family event. We had to throw him face down onto the fire in case he frightened the children.

My contribution to the bonfire this year, other than the Campest Guy in Town, was the paper to get it started. Several hundred notebooks (which were redundant, as I'd typed them up into neat) were piled in a heap along with two dozen half-read magazines. I wasn't sure which affected me more, the joy of seeing how much I'd written in a year or the dismay at realising how little I'd read. There's a fine line between output and input in the creative process. It's too easy to defer reading a favourite book because other things get in the way. (It's all about finding the balance between different types of quality time.)

One of the notebooks lacked the usual splodges of mud and smudges of ink. It was one of those slick notepads that comes with a very short pencil and is handed out at conferences. In it were the notes I'd made while listening to the keynote speech at a writing event earlier in the year. The notes were short, but compelling:

"Charlie Leadbeater. Rules for creativity and innovation:

1) Know who you are and where you come from. *Your brand is important.*

2) Don't do anything unless you're interested in it. *Be interested.*

3) Stop doing things when you've stopped learning. *Never be bored.*

4) It's difficult to learn unless you make new relationships. *Make relationships.*

5) It helps to be slightly possessed and eccentric. *Be compelled and bonkers.*

6) Don't look or wait too long before you leap. *Leap, even if you're not completely ready.*

7) Opportunity builds capability. *Crisis helps you improvise and curiosity compels you to do things that interest you.*

8) Don't get trapped at your desk. *Ideas come from a change of scenery once your mind has cleared.*

9) Have a real sense of mission. *If it drives you, you don't need to drive it.*

10) Borrow ideas and combine them into a new context; say and hear things you didn't expect; challenge conventional wisdom. *Creating stories will draw people and resources to you.*"

Good advice, I feel, from a 'world-famous thought leader', but really just common sense (and what I've been doing in these Journals for the past five years). I bet he got paid a huge amount to speak at the conference, but unfortunately I fell asleep soon after he announced that he'd been Tony Blair's adviser. *("Crisis helps you improvise; leap Tony, even if you're not ready...")* The notebook was saved from the fire and is now safe in the pocket of my wax jacket (which, by the feel of it, is beginning to melt). The notes have given me, quite literally, a pocketful of ideas. But I digress. This was supposed to be a piece about tradition and the appeal of an open fire. Back to the discussion.

It's a primeval thing, fire. It awakens our survival instincts. Early man's ability to create and control fire was one of the things that set him apart from other species. Sabre-toothed Tigers, we are told, cowered in the presence of fire, which enabled man to gain superiority. He used fire to warm his caves, give him light and cook his food. Soon he was forming basic words and Raquel Welch was getting more than an "Ug" in a fur bikini. Man had seen the appeal of the 'naked flame'. Yep. Fire sure kept him warm that night.

I'm glad that Bonfire Night occurs towards the end of the year. As I said earlier, fire has an ability to make us reflect upon the past. It's good to be able to think of the positive things that have happened during the year and then allow the fire to commit them to special memory (quite the opposite of allowing them to go up in smoke). I think of my dawn walk through the wood in January, the snowfall in February, Malcolm's attempts to escape his wife in March, the birdsong of April, the coolness of the wood in May, the sunset in June, stargazing in July and how I retained my freedom in August; I think of the fresh air and pleasure of being outdoors in September, to the importance of 'autumn perspective' in October. This month and next will be spent in quiet reflection and then a new year will begin. A year that should, I believe, focus on the finer things in life. (The sentimental things that, when we glimpse them, transport us instantly to the Quiet Fields.)

There are many things that I've chosen not to write about this year. I didn't discuss the birth of 'Little Lady' Hudson in January; or the bluebells that appeared in April; or the frogs that croaked all evening in May; or the fox cubs playing in Priory Wood in June; or the adders and slow worms I studied in July; or the yellow Harvest Moon I saw in August; or the dormouse nest I discovered in September; or the enormous crop of chestnuts I gathered in October. These are some of the many highlights of the year that are best left for me to savour at times like this.

As I write, three owls are hooting in the oak trees to my right. There's a tawny, a barn owl and a little owl. Each is identifiable by its hoot (only the tawny gives a "Twit-Twoo", the other do are making a series of "shrieks" and "eeks"). Their calls are a fitting conclusion to these recollections and reflections beside the fire. It's time for me to put away this pen, grab a sparkler and write my name in the night sky. The fire's getting hot and it's time to release some fireworks.

Remember, remember. It's the 5th of November.

XIV

INSIDE OUT, OUTSIDE IN

Part 1 – Inside Out

If the Quiet Fields were human (most likely a beautiful and forgiving woman) then how would you introduce yourself to her? What would you say, knowing that she's already aware of your secrets and intentions? This is why I often describe Nature as a mirror. Do you stare into it, or tilt your head to look behind the plane of the apparent? Have you ever walked behind the mirror to see what supports it? Some would prefer flip the mirror to reveal that it's nothing more than a thin veneer, something that would shatter with too much noise or mishandling. A mirror is from one angle infinite, yet from another is flat and lifeless. It's the same with Nature, depending upon your viewpoint. As Woody Allen once said, "I love nature; I just don't want to get any of it on me". Fortunately, this isn't how I, and most of my friends, engage with the natural world. Being an outdoorsman isn't an armchair recreation. If we want to understand what gives life to every natural thing on this planet, then we have to push our fingertips into the soil and 'feel' its affect upon us. Sadly, our actions often leave but holes in the ground: voids where once there was life. We could leave our marks and walk away, or we could plant seeds in the holes and give a little bit back for our pleasures. It's by our actions, more than our words, that our impact upon the natural world is most felt. As Charles Darwin wrote, "Nothing exists for itself alone, but only in relation to other forms of life".

Environmentalists will highlight the impact we're having on the planet (both good and bad), but what about the impact we're having on ourselves? There are 51 million people living in England today. That's five times more than Scotland, Wales and Northern Ireland combined. Given that there are 32 million acres of land to share, it gives the English just under an acre each in which to play. By my calculation that's about the same as seeing two people standing on a football pitch. (If you were on the pitch, would you be standing on the centre spot, defending your territory, or would you be over by a corner flag, as far from the opposition as possible?) A football pitch for two people sounds like a lot of space, doesn't it? Well, it's half the European average and eight times less than in North America. And, most probably, you'd have to put up with a McDonalds drive-thru being plonked in the middle, feeding enormous burgers to the perpetually gaping goal mouths. Would our space be sufficient, or would we crave a 'go large' plot with extra ketchup?

Fortunately for the space-seeker, the bright lights in towns attract people like moths to a bulb, freeing up plenty of land in the countryside for us to find our Quiet Fields. There's plenty of space, plenty of peace, and plenty of quiet. We Englanders do, after all, live on

an Isle of Plenty. We just need to get round to doing all the things we said we would, which responsibilities and 'lack of time' prevented us from doing. (The world is round, yet we're often unable to 'get round' to doing something. In these instances, we become aware that we're stuck in an artificial world with straight sides and corners. A square world, with hard edges that don't drift or rotate, but which slice inwards like a pair of oversized scissors.)

I started this December journal with the 'opinion' that I would not dangle a political carrot (it's too cold today for anything to dangle enticingly). However, I'm feeling the nip of not having enough time outdoors. I've resorted to writing passionately about the world outside. You see, this week I've been unable to practise what I preach. I've ended up back in the lifestyle I promised never to repeat, all because I had to write a report for someone who's about to take an extended Christmas holiday. "Just make sure it's done before I go," they demanded, "and then I'll read it when I'm back in January." So I rolled out the drums of midnight oil, brushed off my best kowtowing suit and poured some strong coffee. That was on Tuesday morning. It is now lunchtime on Friday. I've worked sixty-three hours to meet my deadline. I've barely slept, or eaten, or taken my eyes off a computer screen. But who am I to care? I am just a worker, paid to obey. I did what was expected. But it's over. I've submitted the document. It's gone. As has its recipient, who is now on holiday and will read the report in three weeks.

People say that they 'breathe a sigh of relief' when an ordeal is over, but this description doesn't apply when you've the numbness of having only eight hours sleep over three nights. I think I 'relieved a sigh of breath' during this time. But now is not the time to moan. Instead, it is time to celebrate. The work is done, which means my weekend is free for me to do whatever I choose. I will return home and put my arms around my family (and cast aside the guilt of knowing that it's been my choice to work around the clock for someone I care less about than the people I love).

Meeting the deadline enabled me to keep my job and provide for my family. This is a twist of fate that comes to many, where we have to sacrifice so much to provide for others. We could get spiritual and say it's a Christian act. But it's not. My family have suffered this week. And I have to question whether I really did it for them, or because I was too weak to say "no" to an unreasonable demand. I lost my way, for a while, and got myself all 'inside out'.

PART 2 – OUTSIDE IN

It is 4pm on a Sunday afternoon. I am sitting in my garden shed enjoying a cup of tea and a moment of reflection. Today has been one of those days that's made me smile, close my eyes, then take a deep breath, stretch my arms and roll my shoulders before breathing out slowly. It began (after a moderate lie-in) with brilliant sunshine streaming through my bedroom curtains: a sight that has the ability to lift one's spirits from the moment we open our eyes to the moment we relax in bed with a hot water bottle and a favourite book. (For some, the time between these two moments can be as little as a minute, but I prefer to have days in bed when it's raining.) When the sun is shining brightly, especially in winter, I like to be outdoors for as long as possible. It's too good an opportunity to miss and a classic example of making the most of the moment, rather than missing it when it's gone. So I rose quickly, looked out of the window (and saw frost remaining in the shaded areas of the garden), and then dressed myself in my warmest clothes (a fleece-lined tweed smock being the best of the garments) before heading downstairs where I grabbed a woolly hat from a peg in the hallway, and my wellington boots from the porch, and then stepped out into the garden. The brightness of the sun was deceiving. The coolness of the air hit me like an icy blast entering a sauna. My breath formed clouds of vapour that encouraging me to cup it in my hands (a favourite act, where I literally 'catch my breath'). I did this for just long enough to acclimatise to my surroundings before

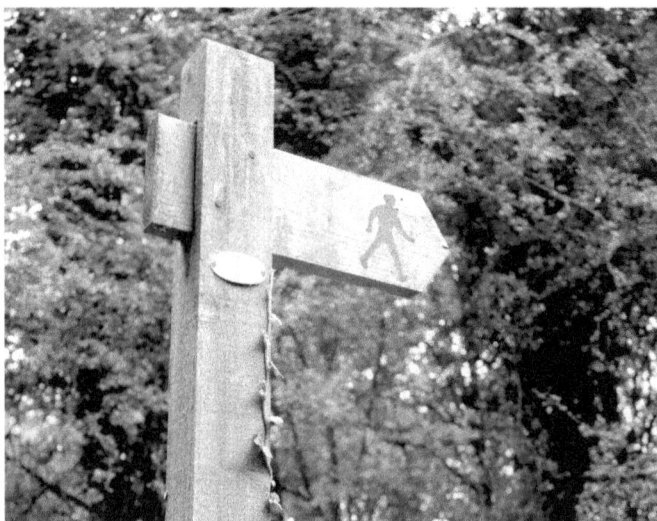

stepping out into the garden 'to be' outdoors.

Finally, I was free. Free from an indoor life. No more cabin fever or flickering computer screen. No more clock reminding me of an impending deadline. Here I was in a natural place. Yes, the lawn was trimmed and the shrubs planted, but I could hear the crunch of frozen grass under my feet and stare up at a faint moon poised in a cool sky. It made the preceding week at work seem as unnatural as an underground light bulb. In a world of metaphor, the scene before me was very real.

I spent today working in the garden. Actually, I shouldn't call it 'work' because it was immensely pleasurable. I tidied my shed, cleaned-out the greenhouse, swept leaves, cut back the stems of dead perennials, plucked a brace of pheasants, built a compost bin and made a bonfire last all afternoon. The pond and water butt remained frozen all day, yet I worked in shirtsleeves for the most of it (although this may have had something to do with the hip flask of brandy that Mrs H handed me at lunchtime). The day was serenely silent save for the crackling of the bonfire, the 'twitting' of a robin and the half-hearted chirping of a confused chaffinch. I listened carefully, half-expecting to hear an echo; such was the quietness of the day. The sun remained low but cast welcome rays. It was a good day to be outdoors.

As I was saying, I am now sitting in my garden shed. The sun has set and everything in the garden is cast in a blue hue. Soon it will be dark. I feel cold now; the air has a chill that bites whenever I sit still for too long. Mrs H has the light on in the kitchen and I can see that she's just put some jacket potatoes into the oven. Next she'll be feeding another log into the wood burner and will be calling me in "to warm my toes and rest my bones". I'm happy now. The joy of a 'homely home' takes some beating, and so I shall end my time in the garden and head indoors. As with the autumn harvest, I shall 'bring the outside in': I will sit in my study and write about the things I've seen outside this year.

'The Outdoors' isn't something 'external' to be shown to the doctor or prodded with a very long stick. Nature doesn't exist in isolation, or at a distance where it can be ignored. We are as much part of nature as it is part of us. Perhaps this is the real meaning of 'bringing the outside in'? As Albert Einstein said, "Look deep into nature, and then you will understand everything better".

XV

THROUGH ARTIST'S EYES

"The tree which moves some to tears of joy is in the eyes of others only a green thing that stands in the way. Some see nature all ridicule and deformity... and some scarce see nature at all. But to the eyes of the man of imagination, nature is imagination itself."

William Blake

Imagine a scene, that of an artist sitting on a stool and staring at a blank canvas before him. He is in a field of flowering clover and meadowgrass. It is dawn and the meadow is grey with mist. The sun is rising between two copses of ash, making long shadows that disappear into the mist. The ground between the trees is covered in bluebells and upon them stands a stag deer, silhouetted against the first rays of morning light. If you were the artist, what would you choose to paint? On this occasion the artist stoops down, plucks three clover flowers from among the grass and holds them up to the light. He smiles. His subject is found. He has determined that the most beautiful thing he can see is that which exists beneath his feet.

The reason I asked you to imagine the scene is

because it illustrates how an artist sees beauty in the smallest of things. "An eye for detail," they will say. But it is more than this. It is the ability to see beyond the obvious, to detect and then capture the essence of things. An artist's brush can capture so much more than a camera. He is like the poet who sees and then searches within to interpret what he sees and feels into meaningful words. The poet and the artist have the ability to capture the moment; that is, how we feel when we experience it. Memory is, after all, based more upon emotion than detailed facts. For example, picture a glass of champagne. Did you do it? Okay. Keep it in your mind. Keep looking. Have you yet sipped from the glass? Did you sense the bubbles tingling your tongue? Did the glass feel delicate in your hand? Did you hold it up to the light to see the amber tints of the drink and the condensation on the glass? Did you look around to see if others were drinking? Were there people around you, chatting, laughing, and toasting someone's fortune? Did you picture anything else? Wow. That's a lot of images, given that I only asked you to picture a glass of champagne. See how much more you visualised by reading these words and dipping into memory, than you would have if I'd shown you a photograph of a glass of champagne upon a white background. This is why I love nature storybooks. While a 'field guide' will help us to identify species, and nature programmes on TV will fill us with awe, a book that talks about nature, rather than just describing it, lends so much more to memory.

There are many classic natural history authors, such as Richard Jefferies, W.H. Hudson, Gilbert White,

Henry Williamson and C. Henry Warren; also poets such as John Clare and artists such as Constable; all were skilled at capturing the essence of nature. But it's the author 'BB' who most completely engages my imagination, for he was both artist and author, and deeply understood the wildlife around him. How nice it would be to view the world through his eyes? Fortunately, we can glimpse BB's world through his many books. There are too many to list here, and it would be unwise to list my favourites (because different people relate differently to the broad range of topics he covers), so I'm going to discuss the aphorism used by BB to begin his books. (He copied it from a gravestone in Cumberland.) It reads: *"The wonder of the world, the beauty and the power, the shapes of things, their colours, lights and shades. Look ye also, while life lasts".*

For many years I thought that the aphorism referred to the life of whoever was reading the words. But now I realise that there's a second interpretation, which refers to the life of the things we are viewing. It highlights the vulnerability and finite life of everything on the planet, and that we have to glimpse it while it's still here, let alone while we are here.

Everything ages, dies and decays. That's how it is unless we 'do a deal' with the Devil or know the phone number of Joan Collins' makeup artist. Life feeds life; which makes me realise that we should absorb as much of it as we can with the time we've got. Sitting indoors keeping the sun off our face might prolong our shelf-life, but what's the point if it means we end up being a tin of well-preserved prunes that everybody avoids? Life's too short to be miserable, that's for sure. Best we enjoy it while we can.

Henry Thoreau wrote that "it's not what you look at that matters, it's what you see". I'd argue that it's also *how* you see that's important. Combine these two messages with BB's aphorism and you have a statement that says we should look closely at things and record not just what we see, but how it makes us feel. Nature books might support this or it might just be how we glimpse it. You may have the benefit of binoculars, or a microscope, or eyes that instantly recognise familiar things. You might have 'the calling' that seeks to know more, or understand how things interact with each other, or you might be content to study the beauty of individual things in great detail (consider the range of colours and textures in a bird's feather, or the seemingly infinite branching of a tree from its boughs to within its leaves). There's no end to the learning.

(I have to apologise for using the word 'binoculars' just then. Every naturalist knows that these items should be known as 'field glasses', which is a much nicer description than something that sounds like putting a couple of waste paper baskets up to our eyes. It's time to 'bin' the earlier description and start looking closely at things in the field, through proper field glasses. I'm going to return to Priory Wood, to where I started this year's Journal, with a 'view' to describing what I see and feel. It will be a 'while life lasts' moment; an image of the Quiet Fields, at the quiet end of the year.)

It is almost a year since a dawn walk began this Journal. Fifty weeks separate the events, so we could assume that the landscape looks pretty much as it did in January. But it does not. Winter hasn't come so swiftly this year. The oak trees still have many of their leaves and the rosehips in the hedgerows are vibrant and glossy. It's been a relatively windless December, too. There haven't been the gales that would usually drive us indoors or make lapwings take shelter in the furrows. Instead this December has been a very 'quiet' month with some very atmospheric evenings. Take tonight for example. I am towards the end of my usual walk across the meadow and through Priory Wood. I'm standing near to the oak tree that marks my exit from the wood. The tree doesn't yet have its winter silhouette and serves mostly to obscure my vision of a pale moon in an early evening sky. Behind the tree I can hear the "ch-chuuk-aaarrr" of partridge in the field, the trilling of a wren

in the hedgerow and the cawking and cajoling of rooks in the distance. The rookery is in a stand of Scots pine at the far side of the field, which must be a quarter of a mile away. Sound travels far, and so leisurely, on a windless evening.

There's a good crop of seeds and nuts this year. At least there was. It looks like the badgers have eaten most of the fallen acorns and the squirrels have had the last of the hazelnuts in the coppice (Mrs H and I have already collected enough for a special treat on Christmas Eve).

Ah, the first sighting of animal life: a cock pheasant is standing upon a tree stump, looking majestic in his breeding colours and clucking at two hen pheasants that stand nearby. Cor! The randy young thing.

I bet he'll have his way with both of them and still go looking for more. Mind you, he deserves to be proud. He's avoided the guns for nearly three months. But then more pheasants than usual have been put down this year, and I've seen some novelty black pheasants too. (Richard the gamekeeper has been busy preparing for the estate's Boxing Day shoot. He told me last night that he's also put down some enormous guinea fowl. "Big as turkeys they are," he said, "not really a hard target, more something to startle the beaters and amuse the foxes.")

I've continued walking, past the oak tree, to where a hedgerow separates woodland from farmland. I can see a wealth of seasonal interest among the clipped hawthorn and blackthorn: rosehips are most noticeable, their rich scarlet fruit contrasts with the darkness of the thorn branches; 'old man's beard' clematis is woven throughout the hedge and into the trees above; and, if I peer closely enough into the hedge, I can see the locations of this year's birds' nests. I'd guess that the muddy, grassy ones are finches' and the twiggier ones are dunnocks'. I'll have to look them up in a reference book when I get home.

The badgers have been active in the sett by the hedgerow. There's plenty of fresh earth spoiled outside the entrances and lots of grass and leaves scattered about, so it seems they've been refreshing their bedding. I'm told that badgers like to eat Sugarpuffs, but from the damage they're doing in the meadow, I'd say they far prefer leatherjackets and worms. Maybe I'll test their appetite in the summer, when crouching behind a tree in the early hours will be a much warmer affair.

The field next to the wood has yet to be tilled. The large, rough ridges have been left whole for the frost to break them. We had peas growing here this year – their roots nitrified the soil – and there are still some pods remaining in the furrows. It won't be long before they catch the eyes of a passing pigeon. I guess the next crop will be barley or maize, as rapeseed or winter wheat would have been planted by now.

The field slopes down to a lane which winds its way back to my home. Normally I can see the lane, but today a thin veil of mist obscures it. By the time I get home my clothes will be damp and the lantern outside our front door will be haloed in the mist. The warmth of the soil is such that the mist could build into a fog that keeps motorcars silent and owls vocal. (The sort of fog that conjures up images of Victorian London, where Hackney Carriages are pulled behind horses whose hooves echo through deserted streets.) Maybe I'll have to feel my way home by running my hand along the hedgerow and keeping to firm ground underfoot? We shall see. Or rather, we shall hear, touch, taste and smell. There's more to this 'looking' than can be sensed by the eyes. It will be a picture for all the senses.

I'll conclude by once again quoting Vincent van Gogh, who sums up what I have attempted to communicate in this Journal. (Just that he says it in eighteen words, whereas it took me twenty-five thousand.) "...and then, I have nature and art and poetry, and if that is not enough, what is enough?"

THE LAST CAST

As an angler I'm entitled to one last cast, a final attempt to capture what I seek to convey. So here goes:

Let me share something special with you. It's a quote by Mother Teresa, whom I've quoted in earlier Journals. The quote is about those truly blissful states where we feel grateful for the gift of life, something she would call 'getting close to God', but something I call 'finding the Quiet Fields'. It reads: "We need to find God, and he cannot be found in noise and restlessness. God is the friend of silence. See how nature – trees, flowers, grass – grows in silence; see the stars, the moon and the sun, how they move in silence... We need silence to be able to touch souls."

The quote leads me to conclude that the more we search for the Quiet Fields, the more we yearn for all of life to be quiet. Not through lack of noise, but in avoiding the type of noise that slowly deafens us. (Noise being a metaphor for the things that distract us from that which really matters.) The Quiet Fields are where life is properly quiet. And with life being a 'thing' rather than a place, it makes me realise that the Quiet Fields have to first exist within us, before they can exist around us. For consider, one could sit alone upon a mountaintop, but still be deafened by a restless mind that worries about job lists, or what people might think, or whether we are doing the right thing. The noise has to exit our minds before it can be replaced by silence. The trick is in maintaining this silence, this inner calm. For once we return to the clatter of daily life, the noise will creep in through the smallest opening.

When so much activity is just 'noise', that has no proper meaning, it's difficult to stay relaxed. At times the noise can be deafening. It seeks to startle us into action, like a gunshot scattering a crowd. But when all is done, and we look back on our lives, it's the quiet times that will have most meaning; for this is when we lived. As D.H. Lawrence wrote, "For man, as for flower and beast and bird, the supreme triumph is to be most vividly, most perfectly alive".

ABOUT THE AUTHOR

FENNEL HUDSON

*"Author, artist, naturalist and countryman. His is a
lifestyle to inspire the most bricked-up townie."*

Fennel Hudson is a lifestyle and countryside
author known for his *Fennel's Journal* books and
Contented Countryman podcasts. Profoundly influenced
as a child by the wildlife books of 'BB', much of his
writing centres on what he (and 'BB') call 'The Quiet
Fields' – those secret corners of the landscape where
time moves slowly and nature exists undisturbed.
But he's also someone who has seen the darker side of
life. Having enjoyed twenty idyllic years working as a
gardener and estate hand, he was lured to the city to
write marketing and sales copy for large corporates.
Here, suffocated by the artificiality of his environment
and the unhealthy pressures placed upon him, he
learned the true value of the natural world. His motto is:
'Stop – Unplug – Escape – Enjoy'.

For more information please visit:
www.fennelspriory.com

THE FENNEL'S JOURNAL SERIES

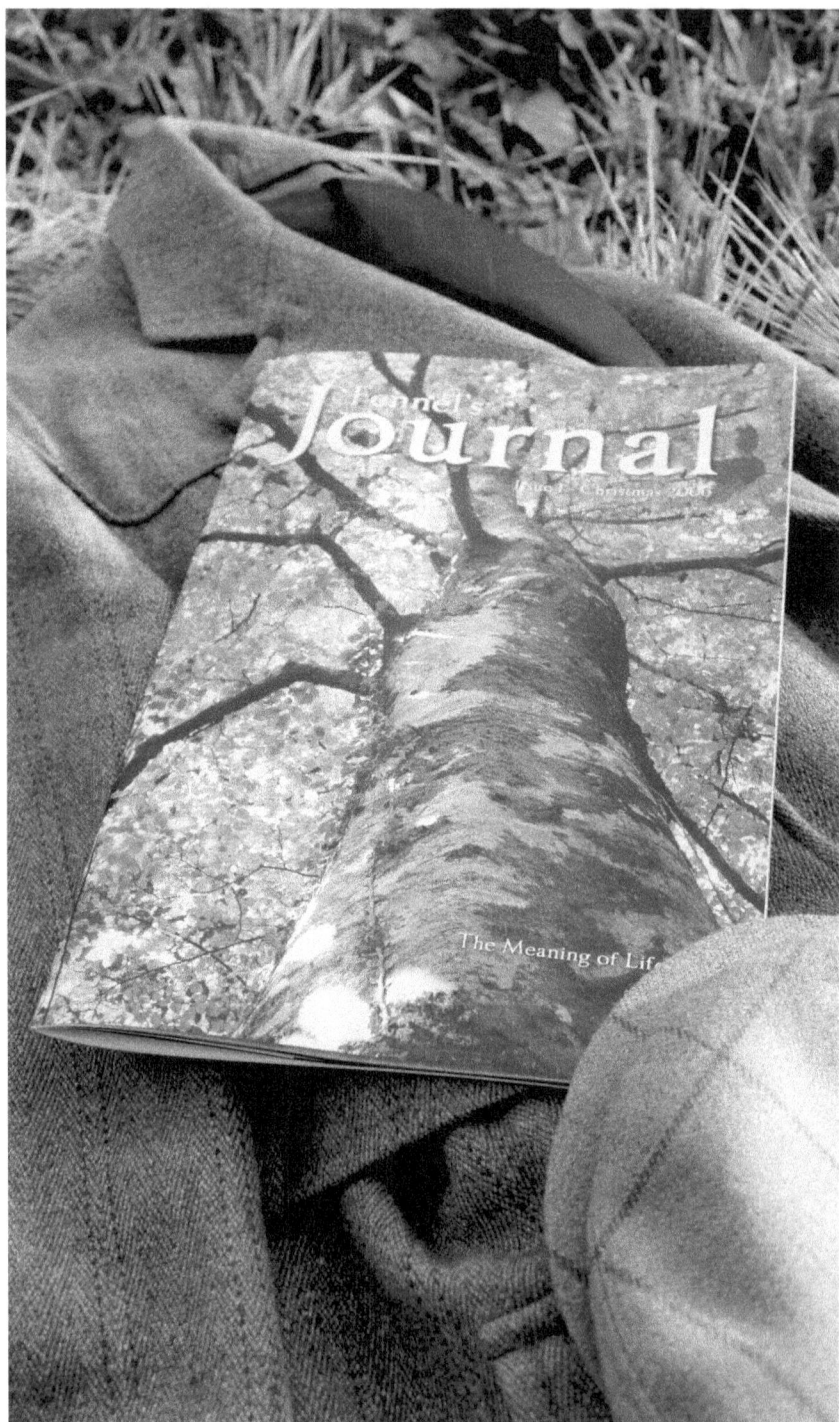

THE FIRST-EVER REVIEWS OF FENNEL'S JOURNAL:

"Fennel's Journal began as a series of illustrated letters to friends. As these evolved they became less a diary, more a manifesto, and the Journal is now exactly that – a way of living, rurally and simply: very real for all those who recognise the importance of tradition and joy."

Caught by the River

"I can see where it might lead. What he has would make amazing TV. It's the Good Life, but in a realistic way. It's Jack Hargreaves. It's Countryfile. It's quality Sunday newspaper stuff. It's 1948, all over again. In trying to escape the present he's inevitably created a brand. A potentially very powerful brand."

Bob Roberts Online

"Fennel's Journal is a masterpiece about rural living. It is a route-map to the life we all seek."

The Traditional Fisherman's Forum

From A Meaningful Life:

"Life is the most beautiful and rewarding gift. We just need to take time out to allow us to reflect, change perspective, and see things in their best light. Sometimes we just have to stop and feel the pulse of the Earth, the rhythm of the seasons and the internal voice that was once our childhood friend. As the natural world grows smaller, so too does its intensity and the size of the window through which it may be viewed."

NO.1

A MEANINGFUL LIFE

A Meaningful Life is the first and perhaps most important Journal. It documents the origins of Fennel's Priory and why Fennel decided to live by a new set of ideals. With themes ranging from escapism, adventure, work-life balance, identity and purpose, through to traditionalism and country living, it sets the scene for future editions – building messages that are central to Fennel's Priory. Ultimately it conveys the importance of a relaxed, balanced, and meaningful life.

READER TESTIMONIALS

"I loved reading this Journal. It's inspiring and has the beginnings of something very special."

"Fennel's chosen trajectory is firmly in the slow lane. He's a countryman, with courage to stand behind his traditional values."

"Witty and emotive, Fennel's writing conveys passion for a slower-paced and quieter life."

From A Waterside Year:

"Water is intrinsically linked to the mystery and excitement of discovering new worlds. Of dreams. And hopes. And thoughts of what 'could be'. Dreams free us from normality. ...As the daydreams grew longer, the distinction between what was real and what was imaginary grew less. Soon I existed in a blissful world of my own creation. Reality, as I learned, is only a matter of perception...A life that is real to one is surreal to another."

NO. 2

A WATERSIDE YEAR

In *A Waterside Year*, Fennel takes time out to live beside a lake in rural England. Here he appreciates the healing qualities of water, studies the wildlife around him, lives at the pace of someone outside of normal daily life, and discovers the freedom that's found in isolation. Getting so close to Nature, and spending time in idle fashion, enables him to discover a stronger sense of self. Ultimately he learns that freedom is not a place, but something that exists within us.

READER TESTIMONIALS

"A year in the wild. How we would all love to follow in Fennel's stead and indulge our dreams, to come out the other side a stronger and wiser person."

"A Journal with a message – that we should take time out to think about what's important, and see the beauty of the world."

"A truly blissful read full of inspiration and humour. The story of Fennel sitting in his tent, with the noises outside, had me laughing out loud!"

From A Writer's Year:

"Writing, with a fountain pen
and ink from a bottle, is the
simplest of things. Yet it can
transport us to a different
place entirely. Imagination is
the real magic that exists in
this world. Look inwards,
to see outwards. And
capture it in writing."

NO. 3

A WRITER'S YEAR

A Writer's Year celebrates the writer's craft. It champions the handwritten letter, discusses vintage pens and writing ink, and celebrates things such as antique typewriters and the quirkiness of the creative mind. It's a blend of observations. It's funny. It's serious. It's real life. But most of all it is written to encourage aspiring authors to find their voice, to put pen to paper, and follow their dreams.

READER TESTIMONIALS

"Worth it for the first chapter alone. It cannot fail to motivate and inspire the would-be author."

"What Fennel has written is not so much a eulogy for the handwritten letter as a call-to-arms for everyone to follow their dreams and make the most of their God-given talents. This is a genuinely inspiring read."

"I loved the part: 'If a pen can communicate our thoughts, dreams and emotions and be the voice of our soul, then ink is the medium that carries the message'. It shows how important and generous writing can be."

From Wild Carp:

"Some will say that searching for your dreams is like looking for unicorns in an emerald forest. They will say that following a golden thread will lead only to a king, dethroned and living in the gutter. This may be so.
But the king was made, not born.
The crown was never his to wear.
...If ever the adventure proves tiring, or you lose sight of your dream, look to the west at sunset. There, on days when the skies are clear, you might see upon the horizon a thin layer of golden mist. When it appears, you will know its purpose: it is the mist of believing."

NO. 4

WILD CARP

Angling for wild carp is about adventure, history, atmosphere and emotion. *Wild Carp* captures this aplenty, describing Fennel's 20-year quest to find a very special type of fish. But it's also about nature connection and a desire to uncover the seemingly impossible – a place where we can discover and live out our dreams, to completely indulge the mantra of 'Stop – Unplug – Escape – Enjoy'.

READER TESTIMONIALS

"When written well, traditional angling writing by the likes of BB, for example, is the type of literature that I can read again and again. Fennel's writing flows un-hurried without overly romanticising each point and the research is thorough; from the first sentence I was thinking, 'this lad can write!' It's informative and very refreshing."

"Such inspiring writing. His words 'Somewhere in the undergrowth of the impossible' had me staring out from the page in amazement. Fennel's writing is pure poetry."

From Fly Fishing:

"The deeper we travel into the natural world, and the greater the number of technological encumbrances we leave behind, the more likely we are to escape the fast-paced lifestyle and stresses of the 21st Century.
For some, angling enables a quest into the unknown, an adventure into the wild. For these fortunate folk, fly-fishing is escapism. Their hours by water serve as contemplation to enrich their souls, directing their quest inwards, towards their longed-for state of completeness."

NO. 5

FLY FISHING

Fly Fishing celebrates the most graceful and artful form of angling, explaining what it means to be an angler – in the spirit of Izaak Walton – and how fly fishers differ from bait fishers. The sporting and aesthetic beauty of fly-fishing is described in Fennel's usual witty and contemplative style. As he says, "Fly fishing is the ultimate form of angling; it gives us a reason to fish simply, travel lightly, and explore wild places that replenish our soul. With a fly rod, we're not casting to a fish; rather to a circle of dreams: ripples that spread into every aspect of our lives".

READER TESTIMONIALS

"Brilliant writing. Fennel made me laugh out loud in bed. My wife was asking questions!"

"A delightful, well-articulated, read. I strongly recommend it, especially to the contemplative, tradition-loving, bamboo fly rod devotees among us."

"A very inspiring and rewarding read. I will try to tie the Sedgetastic fly. It looks tasty!"

From Traditional Angling:

"Physics teaches us that for every
action, there is an equal and opposite
reaction: a natural balance of energy
that sustains the equilibrium of life.
In modern angling, these forces are
skewed so far in favour of technology
that the balance between science
and art has been lost. But there is
a movement, an undercurrent that
defies the flow of progress. There
are those who choose not to follow
the crowd. They seek not to fish in a
predictable, scientific manner. They
yearn for the opposite, to buck the
trend, *to be different.* They are the
Traditional Anglers."

NO. 6

TRADITIONAL ANGLING

Traditional Angling celebrates the Waltonian values of angling: about fishing in a seasonal and uncompetitive way for the pure pleasure of being beside water. It wears its heart on its sleeve and a wildflower in its lapel. It's passionate, provocative and eccentric, written for those who appreciate the aesthetics of angling and uphold its sporting traditions. So, with great enthusiasm, raise your bamboo rod aloft for an adventure that proves there's more to fishing than catching fish.

READER TESTIMONIALS

"A beautifully written, very engaging and hugely enjoyable read. In fact, it's the best thing on fishing I've read in a long time."

"What a Journal! Fennel is clearly the spiritual successor to his mentor – the great Bernard Venables. There's so much wisdom and craftsmanship in his writing. Bernard clearly taught him very well."

From The Quiet Fields:

"The countryside, with its vast
horizons, fresh air and ever-changing
seasons is, by its very nature, more
life-giving and adventurous than any
amount of modern indoor living.
It inspires a love of natural history –
everything from the birds that sing in
the trees to the quality and richness
of the soil beneath our feet. Most
of all, it creates the desire to exist
more naturally. And in doing so, we
appreciate the balance of life."

NO. 7

THE QUIET FIELDS

The Quiet Fields is rooted in the humus-rich soil of the countryside. It's about remote rural places where Nature exists undisturbed, where we may sit and ponder 'The Wonder of the World'. The Journal tips its hat to these places, and to the nature writing of BB, revealing the 'Lost England' that still exists if you know where and how to look. It is the most sentimental and astutely observed Journal to date, discussing the 'true beauty' of Nature. If you've ever yearned to hear birdsong during a busy day, then this is the book for you.

READER TESTIMONIALS

"Fennel's writing reminds me of the works of Roger Deakin. It inspires me with faith in the quiet life and that although I may be isolated, I am certainly not alone."

"Fennel has captured the essence of the countryside – that is, its almost human character. So brilliantly has he compared and contrasted it with the nature of we humans. It's not so much a 'balanced study', more a 'study of the balance' between Nature and Man."

From Fine Things:

"It seems that, depending upon which side of the thesaurus-writer's gaze we sit, one's uniqueness as a person can be deemed to be either eccentric or distinctive. Both, in my opinion, are good...As we get older, and experience more things, those of us with strength of character and a sense of purpose will grow stronger and fight harder; those who lack identity and direction might end up sitting in a corner somewhere, blindly taking all the knocks that life throws at them. What does this teach us? That character and purpose are directly linked to confidence and conviction. What links them? Courage – to be oneself, no matter what others might say."

NO. 8

FINE THINGS

Fine Things celebrates the special and sentimental items and activities that convey our personality. The writing is fast-paced, quirky and humorous, reflecting the author's enthusiasm and eccentric view of the world. But be warned: if you look inside Fennel's mind, you might see a hula-hooping hamster named Gerald, shaking his maracas, loudly banging a bongo, and getting him into all sorts of trouble. So strap yourself in. This book picks up pace and takes some unexpected turns. From the deeply personal to the outright eccentric, it's for those who seek to be different.

READER TESTIMONIALS

"A very fine thing, indeed. Fennel's best and funniest book to date. He is the only author who can make me laugh out loud and cry in the same sentence. I was constantly in tears, for all the right reasons."

"Deep in places, outright bonkers in others. A demonstration of the fine line between genius and madness."

From A Gardener's Year:

"Roll up your sleeves and imagine
your vision of paradise. This, in
whatever form it takes, is your garden.
Keep hold of the image; know it's
every detail and piece together
the elements that need creating or
nurturing, so that when you get the
chance, you can prepare the ground,
sow the seeds, and make it real.
Ours is a gardener's life, whether we
realise it or not."

NO. 9

A GARDENER'S YEAR

A Gardener's Year celebrates the joy of growing things and reflects upon a life working with plants. But it's not a record of horticultural activities through the seasons. It's a metaphor for having a dream and making it come true. For Fennel, who has spent half his life working in gardens, it's about cultivating a cottage garden where he can aspire to a self-sufficient lifestyle. The Journal sees him sow the seeds of this future reality.

READER TESTIMONIALS

"Fennel's writing is uniquely funny. I mean, who else can name a chapter 'Chicken Poo'? His sense of humour, balanced with some deep yet subtle messages, had me in tears. From his 'escape' to a public toilet, to what not to say to a celebrity, this is a Journal to entertain all readers."

"When I started reading this Journal I had a garden with a lawn and a patio. Now I have a vegetable patch, blisters, an aching back, and the biggest smile of my life. Thank you Fennel!"

From The Lighter Side:

"If self-actualisation is the pinnacle of one's development, then it can't be achieved if your mountain has two peaks...Being the 'best version' of yourself implies that you have other versions kept locked in a closet. Don't have any 'versions'. Just have one true, beautiful and pure form of you.
So climb your mountain, open your arms to the Creator who greets you there, and sing loudly to the world that stretches out beneath you.
Write your name permanently on the landscape of your mind.
Remember: you are a child of Nature.
And you are free."

NO. 10

THE LIGHTER SIDE

There's a delicate balance between something meaning a great deal and that same thing becoming so serious that it's ludicrous. (Ever got stressed about what clothes to wear for an interview?) That's why *The Lighter Side* provides the encouragement, humour, anecdotes, reflections and honesty that are essential to Fennel's message of 'Stop – Unplug – Escape – Enjoy'. After all, we can only 'Enjoy' if we know how to smile when we get there.

READER TESTIMONIALS

"The Lighter Side was more than I expected. The deeper meaning within it – and the devastating honesty it conveys – made me question exactly where I am in my own life and what I can do to improve it for my family and me in the time that remains. Thank you Fennel for opening my eyes and adjusting my course."

"The opening chapter is the most startling, erudite, compassionate and open piece of writing I have ever read…thank you Fennel for sharing so much. It did and does mean a great deal."

From Friendship:

"What I'm talking about is proper friendship. The sort that is authentic, genuine and real. Where we can look into the eyes of another person and know what they're thinking. ...Because, as friends, we remember 'why' as much as 'when' or 'what'. Through good times and bad, we were there. Together. That's the bond, the unquestionable obligation that's freely given. It's the tightest hug, the biggest kiss, the tearful hello and the widest smile. If that's what it means to be a friend, or an extrovert, or just someone who cares for others then that's me to the last beat of my heart."

NO. 11

FRIENDSHIP

Written by the Friends of the Priory, with bonus chapters from Fennel, *Friendship* provides insights into what it means to be friends, how shared interests and beliefs support collective purpose, and how, when we're together, we can achieve more, appreciate more, and have more fun. It's about the broader world of Fennel's Priory and how it exists in others. It's a book written 'for us by us', with friendship as the theme.

READER TESTIMONIALS

"Possibly the greatest gift that this Journal bestows is to let us know that we are not alone."

"Like friendship itself, this Journal brings together people and meaning. It reminds us that 'together we are strong'. Thank you Fennel for leading our charge."

"The message (and evolution) of Fennel's Journal is most evident in this Friendship edition. With such obvious themes as identity and legacy, it's clear that what Fennel has shared over the years is a route-map to freedom and a stronger sense of self."

From Nature Escape:

"I am once again seeking an escape, to where I hope to find freedom and connect with the young man who handed me his trust ten years ago. This will be a faithful interpretation of the Priory, a fitting way to mark ten years of writing. As I said at the end of last year's Journal, 'One's journey through life is not linear; it's circular.' So let's go back to the beginning, and rediscover the quiet world."

NO. 12

NATURE ESCAPE

Nature Escape provides the most detailed account of a day that follows the motto of 'Stop – Unplug – Escape – Enjoy'. In it Fennel returns to the woodland of his youth to study its wildlife and savour its peacefulness.

Written in real-time, with twenty-four chapters that each represent an hour, the Journal is an account of how time spent outdoors in wild places enables us to observe the nature that's around us *and* within us.

READER TESTIMONIALS

"Fennel's Journal has always provided us with an escape, but now we know where the escape can lead. As promised, it leads to enjoyment – and very enjoyable it is too!"

"24 hours alone in a wood, with only 'the wild' for company? With Fennel as our guide, there's no such thing as 'alone'; only the warmth of knowing that quiet times are the fine times."

"By studying the nature within us and around us, Fennel demonstrates how to be 'at one' with nature."

From Book of Secrets:

"There's a greater man than me who can sum up our journey, a mountaineer who in 1865 first climbed the Matterhorn. Edward Whymper, over to you: 'There have been joys too great to be described in words, and there have been griefs upon which I have not dared to dwell, and with these in mind I say, climb if you will, but remember that courage and strength are naught without prudence, and that a momentary negligence may destroy the happiness of a lifetime. Do nothing in haste, look well to each step, and from the beginning think what may be the end.'"

NO. 13

BOOK OF SECRETS

Book of Secrets links all editions of Fennel's Journal together. With 14 Journals in the series, and 14 core chapters in this book, it's the 'one book to bind them all' with each chapter providing the continuity story from one Journal to the next.

Containing Fennel's previously private writing, it provides deep insight into the Fennel's Journal story. If you've ever wondered why each Journal is themed the way it is, or tried to find the metaphor in each edition, then *Book of Secrets* is for you.

READER TESTIMONIALS

"What a privilege: being able to read the private writing of my favourite author. Book of Secrets is a treat."

"Such honesty and wit. Fennel puts into words what I have only ever thought, or dare not say."

"Fennel's Journal really is a series – it's meant to be read as a whole. And now we have the key to unlock it."

From The Pursuit of Life:

"We can hide, or we can strive – for a life of our making. With endless possibilities and opportunities to reach for our dreams, we owe it to ourselves to dream big and keep going, irrespective of what we might encounter. Sadly, the thing that most limits our success is not others, but ourselves. How strongly we believe, how confidently we act, how fiercely we react, how passionately we want, and how life-affirmingly compelled we are to grow and blossom; that's how we keep going, no matter what, to be the person we want to be, living the life we deserve, in dreams that are real."

NO. 14

THE PURSUIT OF LIFE

The Pursuit of Life concludes the Fennel's Journal story. It's a reflective tome that provides Fennel's commentary on the journey and a 'behind the scenes' view of the challenges and rewards of a life rebuilt on one's terms.

It's an account of how the series came to be and how it evolved, and includes much of Fennel's private writing, several of the original handwritten drafts, correspondence between The Friends, and encouragement for those on similar paths. Ultimately it shows how the Fennel's Journal series can be used as a route map to a more fulfilling life.

READER TESTIMONIALS

"A life retold, for our benefit. Fennel is to be congratulated for everything he's achieved – on paper and in life."

"It's his life in the books, but it could so very easily be ours. Fennel has a way of seeing truth in the severe and the sublime, and bringing it home."

"Can this really be the end? When dreams are real, we never wake from them. More books Fennel, please!"